Making Remote Work Work

GIL GILDNER

Making Remote Work Work:
How To Work Remotely & Build Teams From
Anywhere In The World

ISBN 978-1-7337948-1-7

Published by Baltika Press
www.baltikapress.com

Printed in the United States of America.

MAKING REMOTE WORK WORK

MAKING REMOTE WORK WORK

Acknowledgements

Thank you to Anya, who works in the other room.

Contents

Introduction

The crashing surf from the ocean. The cry of seagulls. A gentle salt breeze. A laptop balanced upon a pair of nicely tanned legs.

We've all seen this scenario described in countless articles, sticking out in our minds like a bad stock photo. But here's the deal: these articles are always either *for* or *against* remote work. No middle ground. Like many subjects, it's difficult to find a balanced and informed discussion about working remotely. You'll either find an enraptured freelancer claiming they'll never set foot in an office again, or you'll find a concerned corporate middle manager discussing how inefficient his distributed team is.

It's hard to get a realistic grasp on the possibilities of remote work. As employers, we want the best for both our employees and our company. When we're making a decision for our business, we don't want to fall prey to emotional decisions - we want data to back it up. We want informed anecdotes from folks who have experienced this directly. We want to know about the failures and the successes.

It's great to learn from history. But I think we'd all rather learn from someone else's mistakes than learn from our own.

When you're researching remote work, you'll notice that there seems to be very little balance in perspective. I have a few ideas why this is so. Remote work in the modern world is fairly new, and it's a hot-button topic. It's emotional. It's cultural. It's somewhat revolutionary. And it's right in the middle of two playing fields: the traditional corporate world of enterprise business, and the roguish new future of solo tech junkies.

So, when we go out there to take a look at the

empirical data around remote work, we're instead assaulted on both sides by opinions and biases - and research studies (on either side) backed by folks with just a little bit too much investment in their own correctness.

I see more and more articles out there, harping on the benefits of remote work. I think this new awareness of remote work is a great thing, but you've got to remember that the sample is *very* biased. Content marketers, writers, and journalists are some of the most likely professionals to already work from home. Of course they'll be primarily on one side of the equation: remote work, after all, has been their norm for years.

On the remote side, you've got a lot of writers, marketers, and tech junkies claiming that the office is dead. Long live the laptop! And on the office side, you've got a lot of managers, owners, HR departments, and investors claiming that remote workers aren't productive and increase liabilities. Long live the nine-to-five!

The reality? Both are right, and both are wrong.

There may not be a single silver bullet that works for everyone, but there definitely is a best solution for your own unique problem, and that's what I'd like to explore in this book.

I want to talk about the pros and cons of both models. In doing this, we'll talk to remote workers, managers, and business owners who have been involved in some form with operating within a distributed team. We'll discuss productivity, challenge some basic assumptions about work, talk about what "work" is anyway, and explore some of the downsides of remote work in the context of personal fulfillment, business investment, career progress, and look at trends to see where we might end up with remote work after a few more years.

But let's back up, and I'll give you some background info.

I have personally been working remotely since 2011. Like many who started working remotely before it was a super popular trend, it started out of necessity rather than desire. My first internship right out of college lasted for just under a year, and after that, I found myself diving directly into the deep waters of freelancing. Those first few months of post-college freelancing were supported by a side gig as a barista, but after I quit the coffeeshop I never had to report for work at a physical location ever again.

Since then, I worked for five years as a freelancer and consultant, then for two years as a remote full-time employee (a creative director for an airfare company) and then for the past three years as the co-founder of a fully remote marketing company.

All of this I've done entirely remotely. As a free-lancer, I bid for projects and found subcontractors to hire out, all remotely. As an employee, I was both interviewed and hired remotely, and then inter-viewed dozens of new hires myself. And as the co-founder of a company, I've read hundreds of ap-plications, interviewed, and ultimately hired both full-time employees and part-time contractors of our own.

Anya and I cofounded Discosloth in early 2017. From the beginning, we knew our startup would be a remote company. We met each other while working remotely, and it had been years since either of us had worked in a traditional office. Laying the foundations for an entirely remote company was only natural.

Discosloth started out as a side gig by Anya and I while we still worked our day jobs. It was a slow first few months for us as we dove into the digital search marketing industry, managing and creating Google Ads campaigns and auditing SEO projects and developing web analytics solutions. We worked incessantly every evening to onboard clients and find projects.

Things took off quickly, however, and within a few months we were making more from Discosloth than we were from our normal jobs. We quit our jobs, went full time, and since then we've never looked back. We hired remote colleagues, first contractors and then full-time employees. Our client list grew, slowly but steadily, and we began the long project of diversifying and pivoting away from a mere services company into a tech-focused company with multiple streams of revenue. Throughout the years, we've built processes and established best practices for working remotely, and those practices continue to evolve.

With that level of remote pedigree, you'd think I'd be a diehard proponent of remote work. Well, I *am* and *am not* at the same time. We'll get into the complexities later on in the book - it's a very convoluted subject, and not one you can just make a declarative decision on within a few minutes. There are potentially massive upsides and potentially cataclysmic downsides when you're dealing with a distributed work force, and I'd like to approach these factors in as balanced a manner as possible.

Something to remember is that what we call "remote work" is actually the historical norm. Over the long course of humanity, the vast majority of people have worked from home. Going into an office that was anywhere further than the shop downstairs was a luxury reserved only for the most elite. It wasn't until a couple hundred years ago - a fleeting instant of time in the grand scheme of things - that people starting going to a factory or office. With the advent of the Industrial Revolution in the late 18th century, mass production became an employer of thousands, and the trend grew well into the 20th century. The advent of fast communication (like the facsimile and the telegraph and the steam engine) brought with it the ability to do work outside the traditional limitations of slow travel and slow communication.

Throughout the twentieth century, this trend continued to grow, but then the internet happened. Since we were already going into the office to type on a computer and talk on the phone, we found we could do the same things from the comfort of home.

For the first few years of the new "remote work", this work-from-home status was reserved for a very select few - people like regional managers who traveled to district offices, nerdy webmasters who started making good money from running forums and blogs, freelance writers who could email in their work instead of handing it in on a floppy disk.

As the internet got faster and laptops got cheaper, remote work kept growing. Why pay for office space when you can just work from your home office?

And then, the younger generation who had entirely grown up surrounded with computers started to get into the work force. By this time, it was hardly a question of *how.* Today, for the average worker, it's more a question of *why not?*

There are many reasons why a company might decide to distribute their workforce: added financial savings, increased timezone coverage, territorial market expansion, gaining access to a wider pool of skillsets and workers, improved diversity of ideas, better job perks, and an almost endless amount of other equally valid factors.

Financial savings is perhaps the most common of reasons that a company goes remote. By doing this, a company can effectively provide a better level of income to those in the company who live in lower cost of living areas, from the guys in the C-suite to the folks in customer service.

Why do millions of New York workers commute hours daily from Connecticut or New Jersey? They're making big-city wages and living in a much cheaper area, and often their standard of living exceeds anything but the most fortunate of New York City's natives can afford. This is an example of remote work on a micro scale (if slightly inefficient and onerous). You see this pattern in every large metro area: commuting from Oakland to San Francisco, Rockford to Chicago, Round Rock to Austin. With remote work, you can work for a Silicon Valley company while living in the middle of Nebraska, or on the beach in Thailand. This income arbitrage, as it's known, is the single most influential reason why remote work has swept the digital world by storm. If you can work from anywhere, why would you pay $4000 for rent in New York City? Half that amount would get you a beachfront villa in Bali.

Unfortunately, there's a dark side to this. I've seen more than one company use going fully remote as a last-ditch effort to save a dying business. Cutting overhead like offices can be a massive benefit for a company in a cash flow crunch. But this doesn't make it *ideal*, any more than amputating a gangrened leg to save the rest of the body is ideal. I've seen it happen too often as a last-ditch effort to induce profitability in a dying industry, and when this is the case it's hardly the best long-term strategy from a business perspective.

If you go a little bit further, there's an even darker side. You don't see it super often, mostly because it's unsustainable, but an increasing amount of companies use remote work as a form of in-sourcing - bringing cheap offshore labor into the company as full-time workers. This strategy operates on the assumption that you can run a first-world company on workers that cost four hundred bucks a month. We'll go into this in far more detail later on, but there's some simple reasons why it doesn't work in the long term. Good workers are worth their wages no matter where they're from, and companies that try to cheap out on payroll quickly learn that their best remote employees will move on to somewhere they're paid a competitive wage.

That's not to say that it doesn't make financial sense to go fully remote: in many cases, it's absolutely the best decision a company can make. But in order for it to work, the remote ethos needs to be baked into your company from the start, not as a last-ditch effort to cut costs and turn a company around.

Timezone coverage - the ability to have hands on deck at every moment throughout the day - is another benefit that is especially unique to certain industries. Having remote employees spread out throughout the globe is invaluable to companies, allowing you to keep an eight-hour workday but have constant uptime. This can be a huge benefit to businesses dependent upon heavy customer service, high-touch service businesses, or IT businesses in sensitive industries like healthcare, security, or finance. Adding just three or four positions can ensure that the entire globe is covered. It's a rare need, but one that is perfectly suited for a distributed team.

Territorial market expansion is another reason. A rapidly growing global company can't always afford the immense expense of establishing physical offices in every new market, and remote employees can be the perfect antidote to this problem. Instead of spending tens or even hundreds of thousands on new office space, HR, company registration, and banking, you can simply hire regional employees able to travel within the specified area during launch.

Gaining access to a wider pool of skillsets is a massive benefit, and perhaps my favorite. If you're operating in an uncommon niche, finding the perfect candidate for a role who both matches your company's culture, possesses the specific skillsets, and also lives in your immediate area can be a literally impossible task. Our first full-time hire at Discosloth was remote, simply because there was no one within commuting distance who had the requisite skillsets (managing ad campaigns on the Google and Microsoft advertising platforms). Not only were we able to get hundreds of applicants for the position, but we found an employee who matched our culture perfectly - and was actually an ex-Googler, on top of that.

Going remote can also vastly improve your diversity of ideas and operation. We'll go into far more detail about the upsides and downsides of bringing in more cultures into your company, but for tech-centric businesses I can't think of something more valuable than bringing in people who can shatter the status quo. I've worked in hyper-local businesses before. Don't get me wrong: it can work extremely well, especially in a small-town scenario, because everyone works together like clockwork. But any expansion outside of that small town comfort zone becomes impossible, because an entirely homogenous company isn't terribly flexible or adaptive. Bringing in additional cultures can be the spark that takes you from mediocre to amazing.

Offering a remote workplace is also an incredible job perk. More and more, as remote work becomes somewhat normalized within the tech-forward world, excellent developers and marketers and project managers want to work from home (or from a beach somewhere). The freedom and independence that you're afforded with a remote job can be priceless. Giving someone the option to work remotely can be the difference in hiring the perfect candidate, or getting passed over for some other company.

How This Book Is Structured

This book is divided into distinct sections that address different issues in the world of remote work. If you're a manager or owner interested in building a remote team, perhaps the first few sections will be of interest to you. If you're an employee at a remote company, perhaps the latter sections will be more applicable. Either way, I think that it's probably a good idea to look at remote work from both perspectives, whether you're on the management side or on the employee side. There's a lot of give and take involved in a successful remote team. If a single thing is the most crucial element of success, it's independence and ability to complete work without micromanagement. This requires a level of understanding of where each other is coming from.

First, we will look at the details involved in putting together a high-functioning remote team: how to identify individuals who will work well in a remote environment, how to best interview these candidates, the importance of team cohesiveness, the importance of face time, how to identify remote colleagues that aren't pulling their own weight, and then an entire range of potential team issues including time zones, payroll, and communication.

Then, we'll have an entire section devoted to perhaps the most practical approach to actually structuring your team: a remote blueprint. We'll lay out just how we do it at Discosloth, and what we've found works best. This blueprint section will detail things like how to onboard new team members, communication tools & standard policies, and how to focus on motivation and performance as a remote team.

The next section will focus on being a remote

worker yourself, and detail the important personal lessons we've learned on being focused, maintaining a successful career, and how to alleviate the various problems that pop up as a remote worker.

And finally, we've dedicated an entire section on remote workflow and communication. It's notable that in many remote companies, one of the biggest points of divisiveness is just how to communicate with one another. It seems like extroverted sales executives prefer different modes of communication than introverted software developers, for example, so establishing a cohesive and consistent policy of communication is extremely important. We've developed a form of communication triage, which helps guide a remote team into a consistent form of talking with each other while being entirely remote.

Building Remote Teams

Putting Together The Perfect Remote Team

This section is for the manager, or the business owner, who wants to go remote.

There are many reasons for this intent - and the various benefits range from finances, lifestyle improvements, productivity, or simply because it seems like a good idea.

The good news is, building a remote team is easier than ever. The bad news, though, is that it's still a very unknown field. It's not a universal practice. There is still a lot to be learned and a lot to be explored. However, a few basic lessons can be learned from the experiences of others that make the path a lot easier for the rest of us.

Our experiences have been biased towards the fields of tech and marketing, so if you're in a different area of work you can expect some minor differences. However, chances are if you're considering the efficacy of implementing a remote policy in your business, you're probably in one of these fields.

Any business in which the personnel spent most of their time in front of a computer screen is a business which can convert to remote work. Although I have spent over a decade working remotely in the field of digital marketing (all the way from an entry-level employee, to mid-level management, to a business owner) the general policies will apply to nearly any other industry as well.

Who Makes A Good Remote Colleague?

Not everyone is cut out for remote work.

The most positive reason for not being cut out for remote work is that you simply don't like it. And this is an excellent reason! For many, going into the office, having lunch with colleagues, having a predictable routine, and interacting with people on a daily basis is very important. If someone enjoys going to the office, they're not going to be attracted to working remotely in the same way others are.

There are some negative reasons that make someone a poor fit for remote work, as well. In my experience, the most negative reason is laziness. Even

though it's still very competitive and relatively difficult to land a fully remote job, it's easy to not do
what you need to do. Nobody's watching you.
There's no nosy coworker in the cubicle next to you,
no manager breathing down your back, no boss who
walks through the office from time to time.

A successful, long-term, sustainable remote employee is self-driven, ambitious, and hard-working.
They've got to want to work. And perhaps most of
all, they've got to be extremely independent.

From a macro perspective, independence means
owning the decision-making process in your life,
including accepting full responsibility for both positive and negative consequences from your actions.
This is crucial for the remote employee: if they have
to be micromanaged from a distance, they're simply
not cut out for remote work. Taking personal initiative is a basic essential, and it's something to keep at
the forefront of your mind when you're hiring a remote employee.

In talking to managers and business owners, I'm
told that today's workers aren't very independent.

Now, I'm from a younger generation myself, so I bristle when someone brings up "lazy millennials". I know that's a generalization, and pretty flat-out anti- thetical to my own experience. But I think the basic spark that makes the middle-aged manager complain about independence is real: it's just not necessarily a generational problem.

The modern world has brought with it a lot of fundamental problems, most of them psychological and philosophical and far outside the scope of this book. But I think it's really important to glance at the root of the problems and wonder if there's a so- lution.

Ten thousand years ago, it was a lot easier to know your purpose.

When survival is difficult - when hunting your supper is a matter of life and death rather than rummaging through the fridge - you don't have to worry about ideals. When it's you versus a saber- tooth tiger, you aren't too worried about vacation time, health insurance, or compulsory education.

For better or worse, the average run-of-the-mill

swers.

What are the definitely right answers?

First, it's good if they want to work remotely because they want their work to be directly reflected in a reward, like how much they make or how independence they have.

Second, it's good if they want to do this because their personal growth and goals are currently limited by location or employment, and remote work will help them afford both the time and money to complete those goals.

Third, they want to do this because they do their best work when they're making the decisions themselves, and it makes them happy.

Definitely wrong answers?

First, it's a warning sign that they want to work remotely because they don't like working full time. Remote work, after all, is still work. It's not remote vacation.

Second, it's not good if they want to do this because it's *other people's fault* they haven't been able to meet their goals and dreams. In remote work, you must be extremely responsible for your own faults and failures - as well as successes! You want self-driven, motivated, responsible individuals.

Or third, another terrible motive is that they want to work remotely because they are unhappy, and they think going somewhere else will solve their problems. The grass is greener on the other side, until you step across the fence.

Perhaps your candidate's answers line up with one side of these or the other, or are a mixture of the two. But the basic premise is keeping a balance between positivity and negativity: and most of all, self-awareness.

If someone is pursuing remote work because they're an ambitious, energetic, independent person who just wants to work hard and do cool stuff, they're in the right boat.

If they're doing this because they're apathetic or anti-social, perhaps someone whose ultimate goal is relaxing in a hammock with their email open in the background, their boat will start to sink.

Make sure they've got a doggedly hard work ethic. That's really the only way of making remote work work for both the company and the employee.

Interviewing Candidates For Remote Positions

Interviewing is a hell of an art. It's not even a science, as you might think: there is something about a good interviewer that just can't be universally replicated. Asking the right questions, probing for truth, putting the candidate at ease, and keeping a strict agenda is something that seems innate with some folks. I'm always impressed with those who can interview candidates well.

One of my first jobs as a remote employee started out with a series of interviews with the executive who would be my future boss. He remains, to this day, one of the greatest interviewers I've ever known. It was somehow a *pleasure* to be interviewed by him. He asked all the right questions, knew how to put me at ease, and still was able to check off his list of essential questions without it feeling like a quiz bowl tournament.

I've done my fair share of looking through resumes, shortlisting candidates, and interviewing future employees, but I'm no master at this. It can be very difficult to push through your gut reactions and make a perfect hire. And to be honest even this executive, the best interviewer I've met, still ended up making some big hiring mistakes.

I can't claim a perfect track record, either. A few years ago, Discosloth was doing some marketing consulting for a rapidly growing startup. Revenue, funding, and team was expanding exponentially, and as part of this growth they needed to hire a marketing director. At the time their marketing team was completely remote. Although it wasn't under our direct purview, I was invited to interview a potential candidate who had been shortlisted, done a great job on a small paid test project, and was about to be offered a position.

I had a short video interview with Talia. She was familiar with all the right jargon, brought up some good ideas that jived with mine, was friendly enough, and had a great history of experience at some well-known companies. I gave the hiring director my approval. There were no obvious red flags.

Turns out, Talia was one of the worst marketing directors we have ever worked with. She was an incredible interviewee, and was somehow able to put on a face of expertise that immediately melted as soon as she was hired. We met her in person a few times at the company's onsite meetings. She was grating and awkward, and I could visibly see her new colleagues become uncomfortable around her.

It was as if, upon hiring, she cast off her robes of humility and feasted upon her power. She sent aggressive emails, spread blame around the office, deny any problems from her end, started instituting inefficient policies and processes, and completely nuked marketing strategies that had been working well for years. She didn't really have a true understanding of any marketing tools. Talking to her was impossible, like talking to a concrete wall. She was inflexible, and not once admitted fault or accepted an alternative strategy to a problem. It was one of the most shocking about-face transformations I've ever seen in a person, pre- and post-hiring.

Talia had gone through several rounds of interviews, projects, conversations, and no flags were raised. Two months after she started, she had somehow decreased the company's conversions by over 11%. By the end of the year, she'd been fired.

How did someone so objectively terrible at their job pass *this much* vetting? Unfortunately, she was interviewed remotely, and I suspect this has a great deal to do with it. As I learned later, she hadn't fully disclosed the real reason behind leaving her previous position at a well-known startup. As it turns out, the hiring manager hadn't done enough due diligence, and later learned Talia had been fired for constantly picking fights with the previous startup's chief marketing officer.

Interviewing at a distance is so difficult that I actually recommend avoiding it whenever possible, at least in the later stages.

The primary reason that remote companies don't interview in person is because of the cost. It's not cheap to fly someone halfway around the world and sit down with them. But then again, neither is it cheap to hire someone, pay a salary for three or four months, and see a reduction in company performance on top of that.

Meeting someone in person, feeling out their social skills, putting them in an unfamiliar environment rather than the familiarity of their living room, asking pointed questions, and most of all figuring out if they're pleasant to be around *just can't be done the same way* over Skype. It may cost one or two thousand dollars to fly someone in for an interview, but a bad hire? This can cost you tens of thousands more.

That's not a very remote-friendly tactic, I know. But it's the tactic I believe is actually most dependable, and what I absolutely recommend to most companies.

Of course, it's not always realistic to fly someone in. Our first few years as a startup simply didn't give us the budget to do this with a potential hire. There are some additional methods to filter out the bad hires, even if you've never met them face to face.

The first is interviewing through a variety of mediums: email, telephone, and video. After all, they'll be communicating via all these mediums when they're working for you.

The second is have as many people within the company as possible have a conversation (not necessarily an interview) with them.

The third is to have a panel interview via Zoom, with three or four people from the company discussing afterwards and submitting a few anonymous comments and votes.

The fourth is to *take your time*. The beauty of remote work is that your pool of qualified applicants is unmeasurably higher than your local pool of applicants.

The fifth (and perhaps the most difficult to implement, but also the most important) is to *really press them*. With remote work, there is a huge buffer of timezones, distance, environment, and perhaps cultural, economic, and communication styles as well. Piercing through this barrier can help identify the true personality, and sometimes the only way to pierce that barrier is by really pushing the person into an unfamiliar zone.

If I'd have pushed Talia a little harder, I might have been able to uncover some of those red flags. In retrospect, I should have asked pointed questions about the tools and techniques she claimed expertise in. I should have asked about negative career experiences she'd had in the past, and doubled down on that question just in case. But more than anything, I should have posed some abstract and conceptual questions to her. Talia was a laser-focused person, but extremely myopic. She couldn't understand the viewpoints of anyone around her, and if anyone disagreed with her she would actually resort to insulting their intelligence.

It just so happened that in my brief interview

with her, she agreed with most of the company's viewpoints and strategies, so there was no opportunity for me to see what happened when she disagreed.

It's not all bad news for remote interviewing, however. The vast majority of remote colleagues I've worked alongside with (along with the employees we've hired for our company) are in general much more ambitious and well-rounded than those in traditional companies.

There's a few reasons for this. First and foremost, I suspect, is that employees looking for remote roles are generally by default more forward-thinking, open-minded, and skilled than the median worker in a traditional environment. It only makes sense that progressive companies attract progressive candidates. But there's also the fact that remote companies typically don't hire generalist roles. They're hiring *specialist* roles. Very few remote companies need a cluster of office managers. More likely, they are looking for something highly specific, like a customer service team manager with experience in their specific niche, particular CRMs, support software, and startups. That sort of employee is going to be a rare find anywhere, but they're more likely to be looking for a remote role than a totally unspecialized candidate.

Traditional companies also like to hire someone as specialized as this, but it's unrealistic in most markets. In Cleveland, Ohio, there is no realistic chance of finding a local customer service manager who has worked with SaaS customers, familiar with Salesforce, and has implemented Intercom support software with a Ruby on Rails-focused dev team.

When the net you cast covers the entire world, suddenly you have hundreds if not thousands of potential employees almost perfectly suited for your needs. If you're just looking at 30 miles around Cleveland, you may have only two or three suitable candidates, and be forced to settle for the one who sucks least.

What does it take to be a good interviewer? Volumes have been written on the subject, and I probably wouldn't have much value to add to the matter. But I think remote interviewing, specifically, has some nuances that are only understood if you've spent some time in remote work.

Reading body language, for example, is a skill that good interviewers have. It's not so much a science as a gut instinct of knowing someone is uncomfortable, or faking it, that they aren't happy right now, or maybe that this person is genuinely excited about the opportunity. It's very difficult on a two-dimensional computer screen. You only see the person from chest up. Maybe not even their hands. It's harder to hear their voice and catch the tiny trembles or wavering notes that subconsciously clue us in to a deeper meaning. You can't see what they're doing with their hands, or if they're shaking their legs.

The disconnect may seem trivial, but it's not. In an in-person interview, you'd be really suspicious if they walked into your office for a morning interview and you caught a whiff of alcohol on their breath. In a remote interview, for all you know they might be holding a half-empty fifth of Jack Daniel's underneath the table. If even large red flags could be missed in a remote interview, there is an even larger number of *small* red flags that can be missed.

The Importance Of Cohesive Teams

The cohesiveness of your team is important in any company. The cohesiveness of your team in a remote company is *absolutely crucial*: there is no room for miscommunication. If you think it's easy for management to be manipulated even in a traditional office setting (and it is!) you can only imagine how much easier it is to manipulate the company when everyone is working remotely.

A few years ago, I accepted a fantastic position at a great mid-sized remote company. Excited to jump into the role, I started getting acquainted with the company, learning their corporate values and processes, and started getting my feet wet in some projects within the first couple of weeks.

Despite reporting directly to the CEO and technically not officially belonging to any single department, I quickly found myself a little confused about the hierarchy. The company was extremely progressive and employed some very forward-thinking structures, so growing pains are to be forgiven. But within a few weeks a major problem surfaced, and it was mostly to do with a single team member.

Partially because the company had a very flexible hierarchy that wasn't clearly defined, and partially because I was inexperienced and hadn't ever dealt with an issue like this before, I found myself swept into a strange game of office politics. In retrospect I can clearly see the motivations behind it, but at the time I was a bit naïve.

I'd started jumping into some meetings and interacting with those who I was to be working alongside. It was a great company, and since everyone was so accommodating and flexible, I let my guard down.

A particular employee (we'll call him Sebastian) was one of those hyper-visible types. You know, the ones who always create reports, talk a lot in meetings, send a lot of emails, call a lot of meetings, and log everything in spreadsheets. He was master of the paper trail and master of telling everyone everything he'd ever done.

In retrospect, his previous jobs had been in highly corporate offices, and no doubt he had developed this particular system of being hyper-visible because, after all, that's what gets you promoted in the corporate world. So it's understandable. But when you translate this sort of employee into a flexible remote role, it suddenly becomes toxic behavior for everyone else in the team.

Things started out fairly innocuously. He called some meetings, and I attended. They were mostly conceptual meetings, throwing ideas back and forth, but they began dragging on: thirty minutes, an hour, two hours. They weren't very productive, but as a brand new employee I interacted as I thought was appropriate.

Eventually, however, my own projects started spooling up, and I had better things to dedicate my attention on. I declined a few meetings, and that made things get passive-aggressively ugly. In a few departmental meetings, Sebastian dropped hints that he was pegged for the new manager of marketing. He assigned me some grunt work - really inconsequential stuff like making reports and filling out schedules.

Annoyed by this, especially as I technically wasn't even *in* marketing, I kept on doing my own stuff and explained I'd get to that work when I had time. Talking to the rest of my colleagues, I found out he'd also been assigning them projects, in a strange show of macho authority. And then he requested a meeting with me. He didn't show up. He requested another meeting, and he didn't show up to this meeting either. Finally, via our work chat he asked if we could meet in ten minutes. Three hours later, in the longest meeting of my life, and he had jawed on and on about future plans and grand strategies, hardly letting me get a word in edgewise.

Why did I let him do this? Early on in the meeting he said *he* was the one in charge of reviewing my performance after my initial three month trial period.

I probably don't have to finish much more of the story for you to get the picture. Of course he wasn't *actually* pegged for the marketing manager position. That went to someone else. Of course he wasn't *actually* in charge of reviewing my performance: it turns out that my direct report, the CEO himself, was in charge of that.

Sebastian is the picture-perfect representation of someone who's simply not fit for remote work. There are many individual reasons, but chief among them is that manipulation and toxic behavior is not easily detected in remote teams. It's hard enough to spot in traditional teams. Separate everyone by a few timezones, a couple thousand miles, cultural differences, and a video screen instead of face-to-face, and you have a Petri dish ready for the most toxic of employees to thrive in.

In Sebastian's case, he brings to light a few important things to look for when you're appraising a team member's fit.

First, actual productivity and execution. Sebastian generated documents every single day - spreadsheet after spreadsheet of numbers, projections, strategies, and ideas. The only problem was, it just *looked* important. He actually completed only one or two projects in his entire year at the company. His paper trail, however, kept him in the position far longer than he should have been. Anyone more than once removed from him assumed he was a crucial part of the marketing team.

Second, manipulation. It's never good to have an employee who manipulates others, who plays the game of office politics with destructive results, and who takes advantage of other employees. Sebastian's specific tactics were a strange psychological play. He used up hours of his colleague's time, asserting his authority in an extremely passive way that was hard to put your finger on. He also had a knack of playing information against others, by calling both individual meetings and all-hands meetings. Sebastian also tended to dominate screen time, appearing anywhere you looked. We could wake up, log in, and find chat messages, a couple emails, and notifications that he'd made comments on a few spreadsheets and documents. He was everywhere without being anywhere.

And third, but definitely not least, outright toxic behavior. Threatening to ding your performance review without even having that role is a dirty trick in my book. Pitting team members against each other is equally dirty. Undermining projects, wasting time, and pushing agendas just to cement his position as a "leader" is also pretty dirty, considering the company was paying him for this time.

So what happened with Sebastian, the manipulative team member? He played his hand a bit too far and three team members independently complained about him. Luckily, the complaints were heard. Sebastian suddenly wasn't the marketing manager. The next week, actually, he wasn't to be seen at all.

When you suspect that, perhaps, there are some phantom inefficiencies floating around your department, it might be time to take a step back and look at each team member and analyze their actual productivity. Not what they have *proposed*, but what they have actually *done*. A long-term, bird's-eye view of someone's projects is the best way to look at this. Everyone has slow periods, so you can't just look at the past few weeks. What have they actually finished over the last quarter? What project was actually successful? What proposal actually found it's feet and started gaining ground? Which sales were made, which clients were gained?

Somehow, in a confusing twist to this story, a few months later I got a recommendation request on LinkedIn. I did a double take - it turns out Sebastian had sent a long message asking for a recommendation for his work "leading the marketing department." I don't always understand people. They're such a mystery, aren't they?

A cohesive team is crucial to both the department's health and productivity in the short term, and the entire company's health and productivity in the long term. Make sure everyone pulls their weight equally. There will always be high performers and low performers, and that's natural. What you don't want is a low-performing outlier: because someone who pushes their work around to everyone else, and just creates more busyness all round, is even worse than a mere under-performer.

Focus On Face Time

I remember the first time I saw someone Face-Timing on their phone. It was sometime in 2010, just after FaceTime was launched, and a college girl was holding her iPhone at arm's length as she walked down a hallway, chatting with someone on speakerphone.

Like the idiot I am, I actually stopped in my tracks and turned as she passed me, awestruck that Star Trek-level technology was now available to the common college student. A decade later, this seems commonplace, but it's incredible how fast things have changed. I don't think we realize just how quickly we adapt to new technologies and take their existence for granted - even if we haven't learned how to best behave with them.

One of the first things I hear from remote companies is how important video conferencing software is for communication. And that's obviously true: it's a dealbreaker for many teams. But I see a common fallacy developing as well: in the quest for global distribution and cost savings, companies have also assumed video conferencing is a perfect replacement for actual physical presence.

However, it's not.

I have hired people without meeting them in person, and thankfully most of these hires have turned out amazingly well. Yet I've also participated in hires that haven't turned out so well, and after meeting them in person the reasons became obvious. I don't know what percentage of gut feelings you lose through a video link, but I would venture to guess that it's far, far higher than any of us imagined.

I remember helping a client onboard a remote

employee that they had hired to head up their customer growth department. The first few Skype meetings were pretty innocuous. The candidate didn't raise any major red flags, and since the company had really already made their hiring decision, I gave an informal thumbs-up. This didn't turn out so well. The candidate turned out to be impossible to work with, and our team (all of which had conducted pleasant video meetings with her) were dazed and confused at how impossible this person was to deal with.

A few weeks later, at a dinner with the client, we met her in person. Behaviors that had been totally invisible or excusable on the video screen popped to the surface when you were sitting across from her at a table. Awkward conversation you might blame on a poor video connection was suddenly right there, staring you in the face. Personal bluntness that might come from an unfamiliarity with video meetings (which happens sometimes) was suddenly extremely rude. What I thought were attempts at humor on Skype was actually a nasty sarcastic streak.

Basically, these little individual behaviors, all of which were essentially invisible or forgivable in a video meeting, added up in real life to a person who was just flat out mean.

It's not always possible to meet candidates in person. Financially, flying in every qualified candidate is an expense that most small businesses would be hard-pressed to justify. From a time perspective, that can add an extra week or two to a hiring process that might already be behind schedule. But if it is ever possible, and you're invested in hiring a candidate who is with your company for the long run, I can't think of something more important to do.

Once you've hired the candidate, of course, and you're operating a remote team, it's important to remember that you can't just keep operating without meeting each other in person. Many companies, especially those in the tech sector, have implemented annual or even quarterly in-person retreats and meetups. I can't think of a better way to bring a team together.

One of the biggest objections, again, is the financial investment required in bringing your global team together in one place for a few days. And it's not cheap. However, I recommend taking a look at how much you save as a company by operating remotely (either by your savings on salaries, office rent, or commuting) and apply that towards the cost of an in-person retreat.

Having real-life, in-person interactions with your team is vital to growing a healthy organization, but it's not always possible. There are constraints that come along with a young company, and the financial costs of flying your team around the world can be considerable. However, it's probably not more expensive than the alternative of keeping a physical office with your employees in a central location.

Even a long-term traditional office lease can cost tens of thousands a year at minimum. Talking to a small business owner in flyover country, I learned that he was paying $18 a square foot for an annual lease. For the twelve employees housed in two respectable but small offices, they were paying upwards of $45,000 a year for office space. If, instead, that budget was applied towards travel expenses, suddenly remote work starts making a little more sense. Not all employees need to travel often, but even if they did, going remote and saving $45,000 a year on office leasing would free up a budget of $3,750 per person annually for flights and hotels... an amount that would cover at least two or three typical trips anywhere in the world.

And that's on the extremely frugal side of things. At one of my first jobs out of college, we had around eleven employees working out of the headquarters (with around 20-30 total employees scattered across two states). The main office had a rent budget of $10,000 per month - just over $120,000 a year. For a small company that's a big number, and to be entirely honest, it would have made more sense to distribute the workforce and gather them together on a quarterly basis (none of us made a very competitive salary, since it was a startup, and we were located in a high cost of living area in the United States). That's not to mention incidental expenses associated with an office. Things like $45,000 for office furniture, weekly lunches, coffee, the rest.

When it's not possible to gather people together on a consistent basis in real life, there are secondary alternatives which are almost as good.

Video meetings never quite cut it, as we learned in our experience with onboarding our client's terrible new customer growth manager, but it's a step in the right direction. The key is to pair this with many different sorts of communication formats: email, chat, phone, and hopefully in-person meetings as well.

We have discovered that the schedule and format of video meetings has a lot to do with how people interact and show their true colors, and this comes to the surface especially in the hiring process. Having a mix of structured and unstructured meetings can help people with different personalities express themselves comfortably (or uncomfortably, as the case may be). In a long-term environment with multiple employees working together, one of the most important strategies is having meetings with no specific purpose other than to socialize. Spending 30 minutes on nothing other than chatting about your weekend may seem wasteful, especially in the eyes of corporate bean counters, but in reality having some form of watercooler talk enables colleagues to develop a rapport with each other that would otherwise be impossible in a remote work environment.

The Highly Visible Yet Non-Productive

Somewhat counter-intuitively, the more important a single individual is to an organization, the
harder it is to measure their contributions in a quan-
tifiable way. That's because what they're offering is
difficult to measure. They're not just eyeballs on a
screen or fingertips on a keyboard: they're the voice
of the organization, getting things done, making
moves and executing important strategies.

Companies try to measure productivity, perhaps,
more than any other performance metric. It's such
an essential part of an employee's importance - actually getting things done - that it makes sense.

Of course, I think many people would agree that most methods of measuring productivity are extremely broken and outdated. Unless you're running an assembly line, it's difficult to quantifiably measure an individual's importance within the organization. Yet that doesn't mean it's not crucial to the overall health of your team.

Unfortunately, most of these measurement methods are so tied to numbers that it becomes easy to game the results. This is corporate America at it's best - you end up having a lot of middle management punching the clock, issuing reports, and looking at questionable performance stats.

Looking at how many spreadsheets someone created, how many emails they sent, or how many phone calls they made is a wildly inaccurate measurement of true importance to an organization. You just can't quantify value like that. The only time you can really quantify value is when you're looking at the people directly responsible for sales, but that's because a dollar amount is tied to them, rather than mere actions.

In remote work, you have to keep a careful eye out for the highly visible, yet non-productive.

Perhaps you'll remember the fellow I called Sebastian, the former coworker who didn't work out very well as a remote employee. He was the master of high visibility. The amount of reports he could generate was staggering. The amount of people he could copy on an email was impressive. The amount of documents he created in shared company folders was equally amazing. The amount of face time he got in meetings outstripped everyone else. Yet ultimately, even in his mid-level role, he contributed far less value to the company than even the newest customer support hire. He didn't produce anything except paper.

A fellow like Sebastian is difficult for managers to recognize immediately. And this is because these sorts of workers are masters at manipulation. Even his immediate coworkers might not be able to put their finger on it at first, they just have a general feeling of malaise and a profound unhappiness with him. Most people won't do anything about it, however, in the interest of professionalism. After all, if a Sebastian type is smart, he'll never overreach. He'll do just enough to be visible, yet little enough to never offend or step on toes. He'll just be there. A lot.

And of course, in a remote role it's even more difficult. When you're working remotely, you can't just walk down the hallway and see someone hard at work. If a remote worker is focused on some important work, you actually *won't* hear from them. They don't have time to update the Slack channel or send out an email.

For better or worse, most managers with hiring capabilities (which may or may not be the C-level, depending on your organization's size) are a step or two removed from day-to-day contact with these spreadsheet warriors. They just see the reports. They don't have to depend on Sebastian for daily collaboration or actual results.

In a remote company, it's crucial to break through these barriers. As a manager, you can do this in a few ways.

First, schedule some regular face time with everyone under you. Even if ten, twenty, or thirty people work underneath you, if you go weeks or months without talking to them all, this just creates an unneeded distance between the decision maker (you) and the problem (a visible yet unproductive employee). Encourage everyone under you to discuss problems and concerns. The reality is that companies are hierarchical - even the flattest of flat organizations - and most issues don't flow up through the strata to the person who most needs to hear it. It's a simple yet difficult issue of ensuring transparency and honesty throughout the company. Talk to managers underneath you, and have them encourage the same level of communication underneath them. And don't be afraid to reach out individually to employees to find out problems - even if that might be a rogue spreadsheet warrior who isn't pulling their weight.

Second, keep an eye out for the highly visible: the employees who generate countless amounts of communication. Learn to differentiate the merely extroverted and prolific from the bullshitters. There is no productive reason to generate multiple performance reports a week, to write emails as long as mini-novels, to dominate a Slack channel, or to call a disproportionate amount of meetings. Unless someone is actually serving solely in a manager role, and is funneling along an entire team, generating a huge amount of paperwork is doing nothing but slowing the rest of your colleagues down, and wasting company money in the meantime.

Third, emphasize the importance of clarity, brevity, and respect of time to your entire team. Discourage frequent meetings that call multiple people together. An hour-long meeting involving four people doesn't cost a single hour of lost productivity time, but four hours - not even including the prep time and distraction from the real job.

And fourth, having a regular and established reporting process in place removes the need for other people in the company to create their own process. If you've already got a monthly performance overview process that works smoothly, it is entirely unnecessary for the visible-yet-unproductive to create their own reports. This makes it easier to identify unneeded filler work.

And fifth, but perhaps most importantly, establish a regular and universally understood performance review process. Focus not on game-able numbers, but actual results. Say you hold one of these reviews once per quarter - in a performance review, don't focus on tasks done, emails sent, leads captured, or strategies conceptualized. Focus on actual results and integration with the team - how does the employee relate to the company's profits this quarter? How did the employee contribute to the greater team goal? Did the employee work well with others and make meaningful contributions to projects? How many projects did the employee successfully kick off and *complete?*

Of course, sales-focused team members are much easier to work with - and they're much less likely to be able to fake their way through a job. When your primary measurement of performance is dollars, it's suddenly a lot harder to explain away by generating a lot of emails and reports.

It's almost always middle-level employees that are able to game results. An entry-level employee is usually graded on tasks, and these tasks can usually not be easily faked. Higher-echelon team members have added responsibility and larger outcomes, and are usually working in tandem with the executive team and outside clients. A middle-level employee, insulated from outside contact, and having a good degree of self-direction and independence within their job role, are almost always the culprits.

Unfortunately, this describes the vast majority of remote roles. By definition, a remote role will almost always have a large degree of self-direction involved, and this increases the risk of attracting spreadsheet warriors.

The sort of spreadsheets that Sebastian generated were of no particular practical use, but were cool to look at and exhaustively designed. He would create spreadsheets with names like "3 Month Sales Outreach Strategy" or "Customer Journey Study" or

"Five-Part Funnel Analysis". None of these were ever implemented. Most, I discovered, were templates which had just been copied from somewhere off the internet and adjusted to our company's specific market. The meetings, which often dragged on to lengths of two or three hours, had no clear agenda and were usually called "brainstorming sessions". When assigned with an actual task with an actual deliverable, it would take *weeks* to get something back from him. His emails were long and took a long time to parse, but ultimately didn't really have anything of substance.

Sebastian, it seems, was the ultimate paper-pusher. He was the master of being visible without producing.

Be sure, when you're working with your team, that they can efficiently communicate potential problems like this. It's sometimes very difficult for a team member to "tattle" on one of their colleagues. And understandably so - it's not very courteous and it's often unprofessional. Regardless, make sure the channels of communication are open and that your entire team understands that clarity and transparency is important to the company's bottom line. If you start to identify potential problems, it's better to address it immediately rather than let it fester.

One of the complex social issues in a remote team is that when problems arise, they can easily fester in secret. Because there isn't an easy way to gossip over the watercooler, and because it's not very easy to pick up unspoken hints and body language, you might go months without knowing that the entire department really can't stand the new hire.

There isn't any way to solve this other than communication. In many cases, if you don't ask, you will never know until it's too late.

Time Zones, Scheduling, & Micromanagement

Early on in Discosloth's history, back in those meager first few months when we were eager to take on any sort of work that came with an invoice attached, we had an agency client located in Australia.

We work quite extensively with Australian clients, so this isn't unusual. But the tricky part about Australia is that it's somehow eternally twelve hours out of sync with the entire rest of the world. It doesn't matter where you are, it seems like Australia is always asleep when you're awake, and awake when you're asleep.

Most of our clients understand this, but not this guy. Our point person, Ian, was one of those guys who just didn't understand time zones. We were doing two-week-long website audits, not the sort of project that requires instant urgency and attention. Yet Ian seemed to think that if we didn't answer the phone at 3 o'clock in the morning, we weren't working on the project and something was going hideously wrong. I remember waking up to 3 emails, 2 missed Skype calls, and about a dozen missed phone calls, all revolving around a project that was going well and didn't need any significant attention.

Ian was the sort of client that required constant attention. He sought out feedback on every step of the way, wanted us to keep a spreadsheet updated daily with progress reports, and called meetings every time he had a question.

He sounds like the worst sort of first date.

Ian is not the sort of client that you can manage sustainably in any way as a remote agency. I'm not sure you can really manage a client like him in *any* agency, but when even a tiny bit of a time difference comes into play with a control freak, it multiplies the problems a hundred times. Someone who requires instant attention *cannot work remotely*.

Time zones and time differences in general are rarely the cause of problems themselves. They merely serve to make bad communication worse. In most cases where we've seen problems pop up, and assumed it's because of a large time difference, it's actually because of something like micromanagement or poor communication.

Rarely do time zones cause crucial problems. More likely, they just turn up the volume on existing issues. Working with someone like Ian, who micromanages and obsesses over every step of the process, might be bearable in a traditional work setting. In a traditional work setting, more confounding factors come into play. First, you'd really only see him from nine o'clock in the morning to five o'clock in the afternoon. Second, body language would be much more apparent. And third, distance magnifies micromanagement. This is a psychological issue: by definition, micromanagers love control. They manipulate their surroundings and don't like when extra layers are put in between them and their subjects.

Simply put?

Micromanagers hate the concept of remote work.

There will always be a level of importance to time-sensitive projects and processes. Keeping a web server up and running requires attention *now*, regardless of time zone. Getting an urgent rush project done by the deadline doesn't take *anyone's* time into account. Industries like healthcare or finance with a broken API can't really wait around for a programmer to show up at his convenience, Bali time. However, these projects are a minority, and most of us operate on a scale of weeks or months rather than days or hours. If time zones are creating a major workflow problem for the typical marketer, sales agent, financial advisor, mechanical engineer, writer, or web designer, then you've likely got a communication or scheduling problem instead.

Time zones actually have the ability to create naturally-occurring asynchronous communication, which in my opinion might be one of the most efficient methods of work to ever happen. This is when each individual member works on things separately, rather than all together, but combines their efforts in a way that doesn't depend on time.

One example of good asynchronous work is open source software. A popular, well-run open source project usually keeps the source code available on a platform like Github for users to freely fork, work on, and submit push requests. There is little formal structure or regulation about how folks contribute their code: they just *do*.

When the leader of the project sees good code, it's accepted into the project and becomes part of it. It doesn't matter whether the code was written at midnight, at noon, in South Africa, or in New York City. If it's good code, it gets included.

A remote team should work similarly. There are always times in which you just have to sit down together and work simultaneously, but rarely. That's usually only necessary with extremely difficult problems or very urgent issues. Otherwise? Working separately and then spending a little time combining your efforts can be one of the best ways to get quality work done, fast.

A few years ago, I was on a team that worked excellently, perhaps one of the most efficient teams I've ever been on. Of the three members of the team, two were in Europe and I was in the United States. There was very little overlap in either working hours or roles. We all had drastically different functions: developer, marketing lead, creative director. Yet, once a day we met up and traded ideas and made sure everything synced up.

During the few months that we worked together, we blew away all of our team's targets. Our metrics looked amazing, and we were getting more traffic, sales, and leads at historically low costs.

There isn't really a secret to how we did this. We just happened to be extremely compatible workers who enjoyed listening to each other and who weren't locked in any sort of power struggle. The only way to replicate this is to match personalities, and I'm not sure this is consistently replicable anywhere in the world: it either works or it doesn't.

Micromanagement is something that happens as a byproduct of a bad team. There's a mismatch somewhere that needs to be fixed.

Commonly, it's assumed that micromanagement comes from a bad manager. That's often the case. But it can often come from a bad employee who needs micromanagement.

Either way, it's a detrimental form of work and won't do a small business any good. It's a drain on resources, productivity, team morale, and overall efficiency. If you've got an overbearing manager whose fingers are in every pie, every single one of those pies will be half-hearted pies cooked by frustrated bakers. If you've got an employee who can't find the independence and self-direction to do their own work, your pies will be micromanaged to death, and the master chef will end up doing all the work anyway.

Problems Remote Colleagues Run Into

It's important to understand the everyday struggles your employees will be facing (timezones, connectivity, cultural schedules, stuff happening at home).

On one hand, your employee has the responsibility to create a professional work environment for themselves. Along with their freedom to work from anywhere, they also have the responsibility to make sure they can get their work done effectively without disturbing others on the team.

But, both parties have an obligation to respect each other during the work day. While it's rude and inconsiderate for an employee to work from a distracting environment (appearing on video in pajamas, thumping music, crying babies, a cluttered background) it's equally inconsiderate for the employer to demand meetings late at night, to monitor employee screens, require them to clock out for smoke breaks, to institute draconian dress codes, or similar policies.

Especially when hiring an employee from a different culture, you'll run into some cultural variations that are important to remember. Many of these are the same issues that arise in the typical corporate workforce (a German company will likely be confused by an American employee's cordiality and familiarity, just like an American company will be confused why a Colombian employee treats deadlines as flexible) and thus just require some common sense to work through.

Some cultures adapt to remote work far more easily than others. Traditionally cold and distant cultures will have a hard time adjusting to the friendliness of colleagues from warmer cultures, and flexible cultures will have a hard time adjusting to the goal-based demands of the typical remote company. Employees from other jurisdictions will have to adjust to not expect the same benefits offered by domestic employers. For example, a German remote worker employed by an American company cannot exactly expect to get the German legal minimum of a year of maternity leave with full pay…or two year's leave if they have twins.

At Discosloth, we are a search marketing company. We run ads on digital platforms (primarily Google Ads, but also Microsoft Ads, LinkedIn Ads, and Amazon Ads) for companies who either sell products or services online.

We operate in an incredibly narrow niche. Not only is the field of digital advertising constantly evolving, but true experts in the field are few and far between. When we were first hiring for Discosloth, I wasn't even sure we could find who we were looking for. There wasn't even anyone in our area who I thought was qualified at the proficiency level we were looking for. Even if we did find someone, I'm not sure we could have convinced them to leave their position to take a chance at a tiny search marketing company that just started up.

We were forced to take our search to the entire world. And that's fine, because we had started the company remotely in the first place and knew to expect this.

Finding qualified candidates for a niche role is an entire ordeal of its own, but when we finally found our candidate and made an offer, we knew we were going to have to adjust to their expectations. Our first employee lived in Europe and had not previously worked remotely. Previously working for Google as a campaign manager, she had expectations for vacation and benefits that weren't standard for the United States.

Compromise was essential, and we were happy to put together a contract that both gave her a decent vacation package, and a significant pay raise (the good old American benefit).

Ultimately, it's important that the company strive to reach a level of understanding with their employees, and it's important for both sides to be flexible above all else.

It's harder to separate life from work when you're working remotely. A company needs to understand this. If a kid runs into the room during a video chat, that's not the end of the world and the company needs to both expect and embrace the fact that their employee is working from home. At the same time, an employee who never sets boundaries and structures their work day appropriately is only harming themselves and the company.

Payroll & Salary For Remote Employees

How do you determine pay for a team that's spread around the world, with different costs of living? Welcome to one of the most loaded and controversial subjects in the world of remote work!

Do we pay employees solely based upon location? If they're remote, what if they move to London or New York City? Do they need a pay increase? What if they move to somewhere in the middle of Nebraska to save money - do we pay them less? What if someone is from Cambodia - do we pay them Cambodian wages?

There are some interesting ethical questions

which are out of the scope of this discussion, and probably can't ever be clearly delineated, but there's still a lot to be unpacked from a practical perspective.

A few years ago, I had a role in a fully distributed company that had employees working remotely across dozens of countries. Although the vast majority of employees were American, there were also employees in Thailand, Scandinavia, the Philippines, Romania, Australia, and scattered elsewhere throughout Europe.

The company had recently gone through some financial difficulties, a change in ownership, and restructuring, so they were in cost-cutting mode. Almost all new employees were hired from lower-cost countries, and they gave up their expensive office lease in San Francisco.

The company did what is very typical, and paid wages at local rates rather than American wages.

It's one thing to find great employees at local wages, but it's another thing entirely to *retain* them. If they're good enough to successfully work for an

American company, and thrive in their career, guess what: they're going to want American wages. If they don't get them at your company, they're going to get them somewhere else.

Paying local wages works for low-responsibility positions like customer service or data entry. Paying local wages also works for higher responsibility positions, but only for a short time. In my situation a few years back, what the company found out very rapidly is that when an employee is performing well, they expect to be compensated accordingly.

Within a couple years, this strategy of paying bottom dollar for talent started to backfire. Specifically, one of my colleagues started out at a fairly low-level position at a salary of $1500 per month. Great wages for her local area, but pitiful wages from an American perspective. She was an excellent employee. Within two years, she had saved the company hundreds of thousands of dollars, been promoted several times, managed a department, and was on the executive team. Yet she was still making less than $30,000 a year.

That was still a very respectable wage for her local area, but less than most of the American customer service agents were making. Things suddenly got weird when she started managing new entry-level employees, who would be hired in at $36,000 or so.

Companies are entitled to pay whatever they feel is fair for the position. However, employees are equally entitled to leave for greener pastures. And that's just what our colleague did, and ended up tripling her income in the process. This wasn't an isolated event for this company: successful employees from low-income countries kept leaving. And leaving. The turnover was insanely high: developers, customer service agents, and managers alike all departed for higher salaries. In the end, the company was left with only the employees who didn't *want* higher salaries.

Is that the sort of employee a company wants? The idea looks great on a balance sheet, but in reality you've lost your most ambitious, driven, and goal-oriented colleagues, all in the name of short-term profits.

At Discosloth, we've found ourselves caught in the middle of this struggle as well. Especially for the first few years, we were a young and lean startup, without a massive budget for competitive salaries. We were faced with a challenge: do we pay based on need? Or pay Silicon Valley level salaries? Or something in between the two?

I don't really feel comfortable with the idea of paying salaries based on need. It's something that I've been faced with myself, in my role in the same company referenced earlier. At the time, I was a young creative type living in Little Rock, Arkansas - not a place known for an expensive cost of living. During my initial salary negotiations, my location was referenced as a factor in determining the amount. It came back up a year or so later when it was time to discuss a raise - rent was cheap in Little Rock, so did I really *need* more money to live comfortably?

Today, as an employer, I don't want to perpetuate that mindset. I'd like nothing more than for our employees to become millionaires and retire in luxury. That might not be realistic for all, so we have to find a middle ground. We can't afford to pay Silicon Valley level salaries, but we can do the best we can. Retaining employees, after all, is important to us. Just like finding new clients, it's hard and expensive enough to onboard new folks, so I'd rather keep what we have than constantly be trying to find more. Our employees located in lower-income countries currently make around four times the average salary for their locale. Do they *need* to make four times the average wage? No, not really. But do they *like* to make four times the average wage? Absolutely.

Ultimately, I strongly believe that this issue is resolved organically through the free market.

Remote work is a competitive field, both for companies and workers. Only the highest-performing and ambitious individuals are usually qualified to maintain most remote jobs, and only the most well-run remote companies will retain their employees without a high rate of turnover.

When an employee has the option of choosing

any company across the world to work for, suddenly they have a much higher salary range to choose from. In today's market, you can no longer get away with paying a Ukrainian developer a minimum amount - perhaps it's still less than you'd pay in San Jose, but it's definitely not a trivial amount. That's the free market at work, and I fully expect it to continue flattening the playing field of salaries, as remote work becomes more popular across the world.

Going remote can make excellent financial sense for a company, and it's one of the most compelling factors in choosing to take your team to a distributed mode of operation.

I'm an enthusiastic proponent of remote companies for just this reason - however I always hedge it with some caveats. Reducing expenses and overhead allows for greater flexibility with business goals. But lower expenses seem often to be used as an excuse for a barely profitable company to get by. In reality, the ability to save on office space should give you the ability to spend a little more on solving the problems that come with being remote. Otherwise, you can suffer productivity and morale problems that ultimately cost more than office space.

But back to rent.

Commercial rent is one of the highest ongoing operating costs for American companies, with a national price average ranging between $2-5 per square foot - and that's *each month*.

In a survey of Y Combinator startups, the median company had only ten employees yet paid an average of $6,100 a month in office rent. Of course, due to the type of companies typically going through the venture capital process that's a higher price than average, but isn't an abnormal cost associated with startup companies in larger cities.

In New York City, it's even worse. The average cost of office space per employee is a staggering $14,800 annually...and that counts all businesses, not just tech or financial startups.

While this is a necessary and affordable cost for thousands of companies, it's a massive amount of overhead for smaller or just-starting companies. The amount of capital required to start a company with traditional office space creates a large and looming barrier to entry. And rent is a relatively small part of the office equation, too. Consider the furnishings, office supplies, and collective time and expense for commuting for each employee, and you've suddenly got a much higher number.

Nixing the physical office completely doesn't work for all companies. While I suspect most companies in the world can manage to have at least some portion of their employees work remotely, very few industries can actually be *entirely* remote. Many companies still depend on face-to-face interaction with vendors and suppliers and clients, even more companies serve a regional area with physical goods or services, and even more are traditionally brick & mortar (restaurants, retail, service, and supply businesses). While a hospital may be able to shift the IT and marketing staff to a somewhat remote role, it's unlikely that hospitals will ever be replaced by something less centralized.

However, most white-collar roles - sales, marketing, tech, logistics - are entirely distributable, and that's where we will see an increased trend towards remote positions. Companies that operate heavily over the internet are easily transitioned to a remote-centric structure, and you may be able to shift the company away from the office without even a ripple visible to your clients. In these cases, the cost savings can be significant.

It doesn't come as straight profit, however, and this is worth digging a little deeper into. Although you may save both your company and your team money by eliminating the office and the commute, you can't just send them off into distance and expect everything's taken care of. As we've covered elsewhere, I don't think teams operate well under a permanently long-term, long-distance structure. It's sort of like long-distance dating. If you don't see your significant other in real life every once in a while, it's not really dating, is it? You should expect to spend some of your rent money on annual retreats or, at the very least, flying in your team members to a central location every once in a while.

It also might be nice to give your team an allowance for remote work, whether that's a hundred bucks a month to apply towards fast internet, or an equipment allowance since they'll likely be using their own computer to do your work. Solid, dependable internet and a good computer is essential for productivity and connectivity. Just because you think your employee *ought* to have a good computer and internet connection doesn't mean they *will*, and if you transition to remote work expecting them to use their own equipment and internet, you should also expect to pay for it.

Transitioning Employees Into Remote Work

When an employee is transitioning into a remote team, they're coming from one of many possible backgrounds.

If entry-level, they might be coming directly from college or high school and have no significant work experience at all. In this case, there's not a whole lot of transitioning to do. For them, *all* work is new.

If they've been in a career for a few years, they're either coming from a traditional, sit-down employment model, or they've already been remote. The traditional model is most common, and is where most members of a team will have come from.

Employees who have come from previous remote roles, however, aren't all perfect. They can come with a particular set of challenges. They've either come from an organization exactly like yours and will fit into your team like fingers into a glove (unlikely and improbable) or they're coming from either a corporate or freelance background.

Freelancers have a unique position of both being well adjusted to remote work, and difficult to embed into a full-time team. A lot of close attention and careful onboarding has to be given to these freelance sorts, and I say this as a former freelancer who went through the process of shifting to a full-time remote role myself.

Freelancers have gone through many unique challenges themselves, and these challenges can either help or harm their prospects as a member of your team. It's worth delving into the specifics of just what makes a freelancer tick, and what will help them succeed as a remote team member.

I was a freelancer for almost five years. And although it was one of the best decisions I could have made at such an early stage in my career, it wasn't easy. Starting with only the networking I'd gained in college and during the single year of an entry-level marketing job at a nonprofit organization, I began consulting for other NGOs, producing media, websites, fundraising documentaries and other marketing materials. It was extremely out-of-the-box: I traveled to 25 countries while a freelancer, meeting people that would end up being crucial to my career later on. The first year was by far the hardest. I learned everything the hard way. I wasn't picky enough at the beginning, and took every job I could get, even if it didn't pay very much or I didn't like the client very much.

Like most freelancers, it was a slow and grueling start. But by the end of the year, I was making a couple thousand bucks a month and was able to quit my barista job. The grind slowly got better and better, even though I didn't ever make a significant amount of money freelancing. But it did let me have the freedom to make decisions that I couldn't have made otherwise. And it did provide direct hands-on experience on the basics of operating a business, and all the soft skills involved in that: interacting with clients, invoicing, reporting, banking, communication, and so on.

Like everything, there are some benefits and downsides to freelancing. And some of them I couldn't fully appreciate until later, after I'd gone through a few years of remote employment and (eventually) as a small business owner. The most immediately impactful benefit was ultimate freedom: I could do whatever I wanted, whenever I wanted.

Financially, it wasn't easy. But at the same time, it's hard to complain about. I made more than I spent, and did almost anything in my spare time between gigs. There were long weeks in which I did nothing except lounge around, ride my motorcycle, fly to Costa Rica, work on some hobbies, and hang out at coffeeshops. Then, I would work 60 hours a week for months at a time to make up for it. The downside was the income instability. Even though I did *technically* make more than I needed, it was still a pittance for a college grad in America. I would shift between an $11,000 month, and then a string of $400 months. It was both exhilarating and exhausting, and in the end the stress that comes from not knowing whether you'd have work next month got to me. Even if it meant settling for a lower income, taking a year to work a steady job was worth it for the mental peace of mind.

It's important to note that freelancing is an entirely different beast than actually owning a small business. You're not a small business owner: you're a rogue employee for hire. Even though many of the principles are the same, and many best practices carry over, there's an unavoidable stigma about being a freelancer. As a freelancer, you're also not a consultant, which also seems to be a terribly misused word. Consultants in the real sense are tenured individuals who have successfully retired from the corporate world and have insight that saves the company more money than they cost to hire.

When you're looking to bring a freelancer onto the team in a full-time role, remember these aspects that make up a freelancer's life: independence, flexibility, instability, and freedom. The first question to answer is: *why* is this freelancer making the shift to full-time?

If the answer is "they need structure in order to be successful", they're not going to be a great fit. Why? Simply because remote work does not offer a great structure for folks who aren't already self-directed. Many freelancers fail out of freelancing because they simply cannot structure their own work day. You're not going to be able to fix this without a strict structure that crosses the line into micro-management.

Other freelancers quit freelancing because they want a stable income. And this is probably the best reason behind seeking out a full-time job: everyone needs a stable income, and sometimes the existing path just isn't working the way you want it to. There's no shame in that, and I encourage managers to consider the need for stable income a positive indicator for a potential job candidate.

Other times, freelancers simply want to change career paths. While probably not suitable for hiring into a hyper-specific skilled role, for most entry-level or mid-level positions this is also a great reason.

The other things to keep in mind are the factors involved in being a *successful* freelancer.

First, they almost invariably had an unstable income (unless they were smarter than me, and developed ongoing retainer relationships with their clients).

Second, they are used to feast or famine and probably work accordingly. They will not fit easily into a role that requires careful plodding work, day in, day out. They will fit best into roles that require weeks of hard work, then weeks of rest. In other words, project- or event-based roles.

Third, they will want freedom and independence. The entire reason they're applying for a remote position, and not a traditional office position, is because they want the ability to structure their day and maintain a semblance of control on their day-to-day life. Freelancers are excellent for self-directed, independent positions.

You'll find that certain positions and verticals are filled with potential freelance employees. Freelancing is difficult, but it's the career of choice for more and more mobile creatives and developers. Perhaps the most lucrative profession for a freelancer is software development. If you're going to trade your time for money (which is essentially what freelancing is) then you might as well make as much per hour as possible. Graphic designers, video editors, copywriters, and other creative types are also common careers that do well in freelancing.

On a different side of the equation than freelancers are candidates who have already been working in remote teams. Existing remote workers are a different issue entirely. And it's usually a non-issue, as they're used to working for someone on the other side of the world, but you'll need to be careful to adjust their expectations for their new work home.

For example, I worked for an online airfare company as a remote employee for almost two years, nominally as a creative director and head of special projects. The projects I worked on involved content creation, video production, affiliate marketing, branding redesigns, SEO, and other web-based marketing skills. The positive aspects of the job meant that I didn't have to relocate, had a steady paycheck, had some great peers, and a healthy travel budget (I spent this on filming a 40-day, 18-flight trip around the world). The downsides were limited future potential and limited benefits. My salary was around the same as I made freelancing, but was still a bit under market average. Anya worked remotely for the same US-based company, first in paid search and then as marketing director. She managed a small team of marketing employees, ran PPC campaigns, oversaw affiliate programs, and was in charge of analytics and business intelligence. The positive aspects of the job were much the same for her: a steady paycheck, ability to work from home, some international travel, and freedom to learn new skills. The downsides were similar: no career path upwards, and little outsized income potential (that's why we ended up founding Discosloth!)

You may also come across former business owners who are looking for a position in a remote company. Owning a small business is my personal favorite way to work remotely, but it doesn't necessarily mean that it's the greatest place for a candidate to
come from.

Not everyone is cut out to run their own business or working for themselves, and that's fine. But
owning a business - having the responsibility of employees, liabilities, vendors, and overhead - is a step
beyond freelancing.

A successful business owner creates a company
that begins to take on a sort of personality beyond
their own, and the momentum behind this is what
separates that dude armed with a fully-stickered
MacBook Pro at a coworking space from a real business.

Transitioning a former business owner into a
remote team, however, is one of the absolute trickiest things you could do. Although I have the highest
amount of respect for small business, I can't imagine

a situation where I'd be able to smoothly integrate a former business owner into Discosloth. The mindset of responsibility and control is drastically different, and you'll need to ensure that there won't be conflicting management styles.

If you're looking for papers or diplomas that make someone qualified for remote work, you're wading in the wrong creek. There aren't any.

The ability to have a successful and lucrative career without ever stepping into the office wasn't in existence when most of us went to college. Even today, the normal progression from college graduate to career success usually involves an office job, not going remotely right off the bat. It's rare that someone doesn't have to pay their dues to the man, by going into the office for the first few years of their career to do the entry-level stuff that lets them work their way up the ladder.

There isn't a single specific certification that makes someone a good fit for remote work. There isn't even a specific experience or job function that ensures that someone will work out. It's more about personality than anything else. And chances are, you're going to get job candidates that veer towards the slightly weird.

After all, these are people who want to work from abroad, or work from home. That's still very unusual. But it's also a good thing.

If you're looking for qualifications to find in hiring employees for a role in remote work, there isn't a certificate to earn, a course to complete, or a major to declare.

Remote work happens when you're highly driven, independent, self-directed, and able to structure your work life without the constraints of an office building.

Employers who are hiring a remote employee are looking for characteristics that are, in general, a bit abstract and undefined. They're looking for people who love to travel. They're looking for people who are good at writing. They're looking for good communicators. They're looking for go-getters. They're looking for people who are tech-savvy.

In short, they're looking for folks who are at the

top of their game. They want people who have had flexible roles with a large amount of responsibility.

The path to gaining these characteristics isn't attained through a degree. It is acquired through experience, and that's something that only those individuals can create for themselves.

The Blueprint For Going Remote

One-Size-Fits-All?

Every company is different, and there is no one-size-fits-all solution for implementing the perfect remote work structure.

There will always be outliers. Perhaps on one hand, we're talking about a tiny company of two people who are highly driven and ambitious. They don't need any structure at all, they just seem to get things done. On the other hand, it's a Fortune 500 company who's considering shifting an entire department of 1,000+ people into remote roles. It's very difficult (and dare I say, disingenuous) to give solid, qualified advice to either of these entities without knowing more about their intricacies and idiosyncrasies.

That said, there are always many more entities in the middle of the bell curve. For every global multi-national company going remote, there are hundreds of mid-size companies who perhaps just employ a few dozen workers. And if you fall in the middle of the bell curve, whether you're located in New York City or Malaysia, whether you have five employees or fifty employees, chances are that you've got more similarities than differences.

This section is intended to encapsulate our recommendations for remote work structure into a simple blueprint, meant for the vast majority of small to medium businesses. It's likely not terribly relevant for either the solo freelancer or the massive corporate behemoth - but this makes it even more accurate for the rest of us, those who own small companies with just a few employees scattered around the globe.

First, we'll underline the importance of on-boarding. When you're hiring talent into your company, it's important to immediately introduce people to your methods and expectations when it comes to working remotely. This will include training documents, contact lists so they have easy access to colleagues, recommended meeting frequency and structures, how to organize HR needs like vacation scheduling, and how to shift to an emphasis on business goals, rather than screen time.

Then, we'll talk about communication. In other areas in this book, we talk about communication in a very broad and holistic way, but in this section we'll try to dig deep into the practical aspects of actually putting it into practice. This will include how to triage communication channels, meeting frequency and length, software tools to implement in order to improve your communication, and project management.

And finally, we'll talk about motivation. This is a big deal in the world of remote work, since the distance (both physical and mental) can often de-prioritize or discourage productivity. Things we'll go over in our motivation section are financial (bonuses based on performance, profit sharing, referral bonuses) and educational (paying for conferences, in-person retreats, and coworking subsidies).

A blueprint is never truly one-size-fits-all, but I think that you can extract a bit of universal wisdom from it all the same.

Treat it as a springboard, and adjust to your specific industry's needs, history, and quirks.

Team Introductions & Onboarding

Start strong. Introducing incoming team members to your company's culture, methods, and expectations of working remotely is one of the most important things you can do. And, if you've got many existing employees who are about to go remote, it's equally important that they are given all the information necessary to make the upcoming adjustment to their work life. It's something that requires a little bit of careful thought and investment up front, but saves you myriad problems and troubles down the road.

A solid onboarding process is something you

need to have in place anyway, at any company, but it's especially important in a *remote* company since everything is still unfamiliar territory. When you start implementing a remote policy for your company, you will suddenly realize how many behaviors and policies are just taken for granted.

In a traditional office, decades of experience and tradition have instilled some basic expectations in both workers and their managers. We all know (or should know) the basic traditional office etiquette - don't take the last donut, refill the water cooler, don't be late to work, answer the phone politely, don't clip your nails at your desk, don't blast your music out loud. But how does this basic office etiquette translate into the remote world?

It ultimately comes down to the golden rule: treat others as you would be treated. Practically, though, how remote golden rules play out are entirely different than the golden rules of the cubicle.

There isn't a last donut to take - those donuts are all yours. Clip your nails at your desk all you want - you're the person having to clean them up, anyway.

Blast your music as loud as you want - only your cat can hear it. Don't worry about showing up at eight o'clock on the dot - your teammate won't be awake for another three hours anyway. Instead, the etiquette transforms into respect for other, as well as their time. Get your work done, communicate well, don't intrude, keep files organized, look presentable on camera.

One of the best ways we have found to introduce new employees to your remote work is by creating a training guide - an introductory course, so to speak - for your company. Many companies already have an employee handbook detailing policies like vacation time or how to answer the phone, so this is merely an extension of a handbook, with a lot more information thrown in about how remote work is expected to be accomplished in your company.

For remote work, we have found that this document usually looks like an outline of the company structure itself. It details how things are done. Questions that you should answer in this document: How do I schedule vacation? Who is in charge of this? How should I communicate? How often is my performance reviewed? Can I date my coworkers? When do I get my annual bonus? To whom do I report?

Not only should this document detail the company structure, but it should also detail some basic housekeeping. Other subjects it should address: what software should I use for videoconferencing? Where do we keep passwords? What VPNs should we use? What are our security protocols?

For companies with a head count of over 5-10 employees, a company-wide contact list is essential. Create a spreadsheet of people in the company along with their roles, so it's easy for your new employee to know who to contact when they have some specific questions.

Additionally, the larger the company the more detailed this spreadsheet needs to be. Consider adding a matrix with each member's skills and specialties, so that when one employee wants to know about sending out a client update, they know who specializes in email marketing campaigns, or if when another employee wants to know about pricing margins, they know who is in charge of procurement.

Part of the struggle (and possibly benefit) is that remote organizations develop a flatter hierarchy by nature. There aren't as many places for middle managers to insert themselves, so things tend to get done a bit more efficiently. This means colleagues, who are already all separated by distance, can more easily reach out directly to who they need.

One of the problems with this is that certain employees can befuddle the process and bog down other employees with meaningless work. One of the benefits, if harnessed correctly, is that a flatter hierarchy speeds things up and removes dead weight from the equation. This is entirely up to your organization, however, and depends upon the amount of teams and departments in your company.

In general, we don't recommend too many

meetings to maintain productive remote work. At the very least, meetings are something that should be minimized rather than maximized. The sole exception is during the first couple weeks of an employee's tenure at your company, and we recommend daily meetings at a minimum.

The purpose of these meetings is to familiarize the employee with the company's culture and structure, and above all to introduce them to others within the company. Fostering personal relationships and familiarity with others is vital to the long-term health of both the company and the employee. During these introductory meetings, it's good to bring in as many colleagues as possible.

As a manager, there are multiple reasons why this is so important. First, you get to see directly how your new employee works within your organization. Second, you can ensure that they are getting all the information (both from a practical standpoint and a cultural standpoint) that is critical to their ongoing success in their role. And third, you can immediately identify any potential future problems -

especially interpersonal friction that might pop up between this person and others within the company.

We usually recommended having daily meetings for the first two to four weeks, adjustable according to the role and the employee's ability to adapt. Make sure to leave room at the end of every meeting for the employee to ask questions and receive feedback on points that pique their curiosity. The meetings should be informal and not too long, perhaps thirty minutes to one hour at most.

During the course of hiring, and then immediately following the employee's first day, it's crucial to set the appropriate expectations.

These expectations can't be the same expectations a company would have for employees that come into a traditional office every morning. And that's actually a critical differentiator that both the employee and you, as a manager, have to embrace.

Right now, remote work is still a relatively uncommon feature for a company. Getting a good job that is totally remote is still competitive and fairly rare. Because of this, companies have high standards for what they expect from an employee, and employees have high standards for what they expect from a company.

In order to do well in a remote role, a person needs to be extremely well motivated, have a doggedly hard work ethic, and have an outsized amount of personal independence and creativity. If someone lacks these attributes, it's hard enough to manage them in a traditional setting, much less a remote one. Someone who needs constant hand-holding is *not going to thrive* in a remote role.

At the same time, you cannot hire an excellent remote employee and expect to treat them just like any other person. You will likely need to give them a significant amount of independence - letting them set their own hours and giving them a wide rein on their projects and responsibilities. In all likelihood, this employee did not choose a remote role to get a huge pay bump or a career boost (these are both things that remote work doesn't exactly have a great reputation for at the moment). They likely chose to pursue a remote role in order to have greater personal independence and a flexible work environment, and to be surrounded by a progressive culture and, probably, work on unusual or innovative projects. In response to this, it's important to identify *why* an employee is going remote, and cater to those needs.

Setting goals should be about deliverables and results, not about how many hours they put in staring at the screen. The whole reason you're switching to remote work, after all, is because the traditional method of work is broken in many aspects.

When we started Discosloth, both Anya and I had years of experience working in other companies, both remote and traditional, and we were adamant of a few things we'd never do in our new startup. One of those was tracking employee hours. Granted, we operate in a technical field that attracts driven and tech-savvy individuals, so we have the luxury of being in good company by default. From a full-time employee, we do not expect forty hours of work a week. That is irrelevant. We simply expect results that correlate with a full-time employee. If it takes them two hours a week to deliver amazing results, that's beautiful. If it takes them eighty hours a week to deliver those same results, that's just fine as well. The *results* are what we're looking for, not the time in which someone's butt has warmed a chair.

This approach is nontraditional and makes many more conservative companies squirm a bit, but it's the approach that makes the most sense from a remote company. We've seen the absolute opposite approach being taken, and it seems disastrous: companies that install screen monitoring apps on their employee's computers, require employees to clock in and clock out, or even put performance-measuring quotas on things like the number of Slack messages sent, emails replied to, or documents created. I can't think of anything more destructive to your company's culture, and ultimately your company's productivity. No self-respecting, ambitious employee will stick with your remote company if you treat them like a factory assembly line.

In the same vein, it's good to be clear about how you parse and analyze performance. Detail very clearly how often you will review their performance, and how you calculate that performance. This doesn't mean you have to directly tie 100% of their compensation to their performance, or that you really *need* a numerical score associated with how well they're doing (after all, very few roles can be quantitatively assessed like this). It just means that you need to have direct, results-focused discussions on a regular basis, and communicate how this affects their job as a whole.

Finding Remote Candidates

So your company is going remote.

Ideally, you'll be transitioning existing employees into remote roles, but eventually you will want to hire from outside the company.

This is one of the trickiest problems you will run into, and you're now competing with a world of VC-funded tech companies, New York City and San Francisco-based startups offering stratospheric salaries, and some of the most adaptable and tech-savvy candidates ever spawned on this earth.

There are a few ways you'll be able to start getting applications in your inbox, and these primarily involve remote job boards, traditional job postings, and your existing network.

Your existing network is by far the highest quality method of finding a good employee, but it depends greatly upon just how professionally established your company and your current employees are. If you've got a few team members and a solid work history, it won't be hard to start getting the word out.

Referrals from within your company are an automatic filter that almost certainly ensure the candidates will be a good fit with your company's culture. Team members typically recommend people they would be comfortable working with, and in order to avoid embarrassment they'll usually refrain from recommending people with drastic problems. Having a job referral incentive program can help encourage your team members to recommend quality candidates: we've seen companies offer anything from $500 to $5000 to employees that recommend a candidate who ends up getting hired.

Remote job boards are extremely popular, and

generally provide you with fairly relevant applicants. We've used remote job boards when hiring for Discosloth, and saw the most technically relevant applicants from these channels. However, the downside is that posting can be expensive (usually around $300 per listing) and are really only good for technical roles like software developers.

Traditional job posting boards are cheaper, and much more high volume. The quality of applicants from channels like Indeed or Monster are questionable at best, especially if you are hiring for a role that requires specific skills or experience. The cost is free to slim, but you will soon be engulfed with a never-ending deluge of applicants from every place imaginable in the world.

When Discosloth hired our first employee, we thought, at first, it would be easy to find who we needed. We have the entire world at our disposal, right? It turns out, it was harder rather than easier. We were now competing with companies across the world for a very specific skillset. We tried all of the channels we could think of: specialized remote job boards, traditional job postings, and inquiries within our network.

Remote job boards didn't give us many applicants we were satisfied with. We were looking for an entry-level Google Ads specialist, which doesn't sound like too difficult of a role to fill. And it's a tech-focused marketing role, which is perfect for remote work. The variety of applicants, however, was wildly confusing. I had an application from a fellow in California who made his salary demand up front in his cover letter. I appreciated his initiative, but he demanded $182,000 a year for a clearly entry-level job, so we took a hard pass on that one. I had a slew of applicants who seemed like potentially good cultural fits, but the majority didn't have the specific skills we were looking for.

Traditional job postings were quite the experience. We posted the job on Indeed, and within a week had over 300 applicants. And then the job posting got syndicated, so more and more sites picked it up. That was a few years ago, and we're still getting applicants for that original position *to this day*. The problem was that, out of all of these hundreds of applicants perhaps five or ten were actually relevant. We looked at a resume of a pharmacist in Hawaii, a grocery store cashier in Ohio, an insurance salesman in Kansas, and everyone else from interior designers, telemarketers, professors, and landscapers.

In the end, after weeks of searching fruitlessly, I decided I'd need to hire manually. Off to LinkedIn I went, and painstakingly searched for applicants who were as close to what we wanted as possible. I narrowed down the entire world to around forty potential candidates, and sent each of them a personal message. Out of all forty, only five responded. Three were not interested, one was actively looking for a job, and one already had a job but might be interested.

The first candidate, who was looking for a job, corresponded with us a bit and then showed up to our first virtual interview, just to announce she'd already accepted another job (thanks for your time, an email would have worked). I think she was looking for an offer to negotiate with her other job, but I didn't feel like indulging her. The next candidate was the perfect fit, and we entered into negotiations which eventually convinced her to leave her current job and move to Discosloth.

That's the process of hiring that we first experienced, and it hasn't changed much for most smaller remote companies since then. Of course new companies like us have to be pickier about hires, as salaries are the most significant part of our capital expenditure. Expect to spend weeks, if not months, on finding the appropriate candidate, especially if you're hiring for a crucial or technical role.

Communication Tools & Standards

Having a clear and defined communication structure is essential to the health of a remote company. I'd say that, actually, it trumps almost everything else when it comes to making or breaking the success rate of going remote.

We'll cover the details of how we triage communications in a dedicated chapter, but the basics are fairly straightforward to adopt.

The first thing to realize and acknowledge is that everyone has different communication styles, and therefore everyone in a team has to learn to compromise their desired style and integrate into a common standard, for the sake of cohesiveness and basic teamwork. It is never easy to gain total adoption of a communication structure, but it's essential in order to retain any semblance of organization and productivity.

Unless your team members have an unprecedented level of familiarity and common communication preferences, you'll need to gently force adoption of your established communication protocol. We triage communications through three channels: chat, email, and meetings. Chat is for immediate needs and questions that need a response within the hour, but aren't crucial enough to bankrupt the company or lose a sale. Email is for questions that need a response within 1-2 days and probably deserve a longer, in-depth response of several paragraphs (this can be bigger plans, scheduling events, discussing strategies, or anything that probably needs persistent documentation). Calling a meeting should be one of the rarest things that ever happens in a remote company. Meetings are for things that need an answer now. Meetings (whether a phone call or a videochat) that aren't regularly scheduled are for damage control or in-depth brainstorming for an immediate issue.

We suggest getting your entire team used to this process of triaging their communication. The tools involved don't really matter so much as the way you use them: chat is chat, whether it's Slack, Google chat, or old-fashioned SMS. There will always be folks who prefer one form of communication over another: perhaps it's a software engineer who prefers Slack over email, or perhaps it's the sales guys who are always on the phone and sending email but never use chat. The key is to blend everyone together into a consistency that ensures everyone who needs the right information has access to it when they need it - even if it means picking up the phone, when you hate talking on the phone.

Here's why triaging works best, in our experience in various companies. Instead of having constant meetings, it's easier and faster just to chat through your preferred method if you have a small question, or if you want to check in on something.

It's best to use chat within normal working hours for the recipient (no employee wants to get an accidental loud notification on their phone at 4am). Chat should typically be used in situations where the recipient can respond either in live time, or within an hour or so.

For questions that need careful responses, or tasks with more details, or when the recipient is asleep, use email. It's long been an assumption in the corporate world that important business emails should be responded to within a day, and we feel like this is an appropriate timeframe. Even if it's not a full answer, a good policy is to have colleagues reply with a "got this, will respond in more details later" sort of response to let the sender know that the message is on their radar. It's important, however, to not abuse email. Sending dozens of emails just clogs up inboxes and is difficult for the recipient to wade through, so reserve it for important issues and discussions that need time to think about, reflect, and respond to with carefully thought-out paragraphs. Email isn't chat. It's a letter, and as such is best avoided when the subject is super urgent.

For meetings, when you've got an urgent issue at hand it is often best to have a video conference with the other parties. As remote work doesn't allow for the same interpersonal connections that a traditional office does, video is very important to keep it as personal as possible. Most video conferencing tools allow you to share screens, which is very helpful in a technical setting when you have an issue that you cannot easily explain in words.

Of course, video conferencing doesn't always work if someone is on the road or if you aren't in a setting that is conducive to video: driving, in an airport, or a coffeeshop, for example. It's usually not very courteous to hold a video chat in a coffeeshop, so in this case you should easily be able to pick up the phone and step outside for an important talk. Often decisions can be made much more quickly when you simply pick up the phone or turn on Zoom and work through something face-to-face.

Our rule of thumb for meetings: less is more.

If you can structure your company so that you never have to endure a single meeting, you've hit the motherlode. Unfortunately, this is hardly possible or realistic, so the goal should be to reduce the amount of unproductive dead time (also known as meetings) as humanly possible.

When you're dealing with a remote team, the rules change. In the office, it's easier to schedule meetings. Just pick a time between nine to five, and that's the time in which everyone will be available. In remote work, especially across different time zones, this is no longer applicable.

It's important to remember that not everyone likes working early mornings or nights. And since you've established remote work as an official policy, it doesn't really make sense to require all work to be done on a single time zone's schedule - that sort of kills the entire purpose of asynchronous, distributed work, doesn't it?

It's unreasonable to expect your employees on the other side of the world to keep the same daylight hours as you do, so a significant amount of time flexibility is needed. It's not unreasonable, however, to require at least two hours of overlap. This is a common tactic in remote teams with members on all sides of the world, because it's usually fairly easy to accomplish: early morning on the Pacific Coast will be mid-day on the East Coast, and early evening in Europe.

The other hidden benefit of requiring only a couple hours of overlap is that it forces a limited amount of meetings. It time-boxes everything, and that's usually a good thing when it comes to video conferencing or phone calls.

Depending on where you're coming from the corporate world, you've likely had regularly scheduled meetings at various frequencies: daily, weekly, monthly, quarterly. This doesn't work the same in the remote world.

Although you might end up having daily meetings in your company, they shouldn't be expected or scheduled. After all, a meeting doesn't just last thirty minutes. It starts a few minutes before the scheduled meeting, as people prepare and wind down everything else they're working on, it lasts for the thirty minutes scheduled in the calendar, and then it lasts for a few minutes afterwards while people get back in their flow and pick up whatever they dropped to attend the meeting.

We don't recommend regularly scheduled daily meetings, and if they end up being necessary after all, keep them very short and don't use them for micro-management. They should be at most fifteen minutes long, and focus on the team's connections and understanding where everybody else is at on a holistic level - not in dictating every step of the day.

When you're first onboarding a new employee, daily meetings are probably necessary, but as soon as they're settled in, give them breathing room to start orchestrating their own work days and being responsible on their own time. The first month or so should be used for training, and helping set expectations and goals for the new employee.

Weekly meetings are perhaps the best option for ongoing, regularly scheduled meetings. We found that a one-hour Monday morning meeting, with the purpose of discussing big-picture ideas and current problems, and a time for the manager to coach the employee in difficult areas, is usually the best approach.

Depending on the size of the team and the breadth of your company's projects, a monthly or quarterly meeting may be useful. In this case, discussing new big projects, or overarching company goals, is important. It's also the perfect time to get employees in different departments, who may not otherwise interact, to see what others in the organization are working on.

Of course, performance reviews should almost always be performed on a regular basis, and these are always best done in a video format.

You'll always have urgent issues pop up that need a meeting called. Sometimes things may need rapid, instant discussion. These are unavoidable and crucial, especially in the event of a big project or unforeseen issues. Keep your meetings time-boxed, don't feel afraid to redirect the conversation if it starts to wander, and make sure to respect the time of all those involved.

It's good to codify meeting etiquette in some manner - and this should revolve around respecting the time of others. If someone doesn't need to be in a meeting, others shouldn't require them to be in it. If someone wants to leave a meeting, they should be able to whenever they want. We've seen some colleagues go invite-happy on meeting times, clicking down the contact list until half of the company is scheduled to show up to chat about something unimportant. Don't do this - and don't encourage your employees to do it, either.

Motivation & Performance

We've all had those days when you just don't want to get out of bed. Everyone needs motivation - but you'll need it even more when working from home.

The brilliant Nassim Nicholas Taleb once said, in his book *Skin In The Game*, that "what matters isn't what a person has or doesn't have; it is what he or she is afraid of losing." In short, give every one of your remote team members an excellent experience working in your company, and the performance will be forthcoming.

Creating opportunities for your employees to be

comfortable, and to be able to continue improving themselves, is crucial to a sustainable and productive remote policy. While working remotely is generally extremely productive, things can easily fall through the cracks, and a few small steps can go a long ways in making your team feel more comfortable working hard towards their goals.

We have found that some of the most important motivational policies directly address a few glaring challenges of remote work. Namely? The social aspects, the financial aspects, and the career aspects. If remote work has any downsides, it's that it can be personally isolating, pay less than the equivalent traditional roles, and potentially harm a worker's long-term career aspects because of less networking and growth abilities. Any policy that attempts to counteract these will be welcomed into an organization!

To address the social aspects of remote work, there's a plethora of available options. One of the first things we instituted at Discosloth, when we started hiring for remote roles, was a coworking/coffeeshop stipend. This covers either a membership at a local coworking space, or the purchase of a few drinks at a local coffeeshop each day - to be used at the employee's discretion.

We also encourage attendance at industry conferences. We think that this is an important part both in ongoing training (who doesn't want your employees familiar with the latest industry trends?) and also in creating a networking opportunity for them. Sponsoring attendance for even a single conference per year is a great motivational perk.

Other policies we've seen remote companies institute include free books (for example, purchasing up to $50 of books a month for an employee to read). I'm particularly fond of this one, as it's a low-cost but engaging policy which will also show managers the books their employees are interested in - and perhaps where their skills and interests of growth lie.

We also think that face-to-face meetings between all members of your team is crucial: and, if possible, this should happen at least once a year. This is one of the first ideas that remote companies throw out the door, because it's expensive to put a butt in an airplane seat. But keeping your interaction totally remote is short-sighted, in our opinion. As much as video conferencing enables us to work remotely, it's still a sub-par form of communication. Real bonds are created when you're at a table sitting across from a real-life, flesh-and-blood colleague. A team that's eaten a great meal and gotten tipsy together will do a lot more for each other, and feel better about the company's work as well.

But it's not just about social and career aspects - it's also about the financial aspects.

It pains most corporate spreadsheet warriors to hear it, but your team isn't working with you because they love you. Or because they believe in your mission. Or because they want to change the world.

Your team is working with you because *they need an income*. As altruistic and well-meaning as your company and colleagues may be, the world isn't a charity. Making rent, paying bills, and saving for retirement is more important for your employees rather than just the privilege of being part of your team.

That's why it's important to recognize and encourage this. You're employing unorthodox, outside-the-box remote workers, and chances are they're among the most ambitious and well-performing individuals in their field. Not just anyone can compete for a remote position, so they deserve to be rewarded for their expertise. If you provide everything else, but forget to reward them handsomely with cash, you're going to see an insane amount of churn.

Many companies use a recognition and reward system. This is a great idea, but it can't be divorced totally from financial reward. Although it's nice to be "employee of the quarter", it doesn't mean much to your employees once they've lost that brief flash of dopamine. Having some form of financial reward attached, even if it's a small amount, means infinitely more than a fancy title.

We encourage a holiday bonus system. Our team is scattered across the United States and Europe, so we provide an annual bonus around Christmas. The amount changes according to performance and how well the company has done that year, but the amount can be anywhere from a small gift to a full "13th salary", a popular form of bonus in Europe which is an extra month's salary given at the end of the year.

Profit sharing is another popular incentive. I love the *idea* of profit sharing. In practice I haven't seen it implemented very well. Like most numbers, the mathematical gymnastics involved in calculating profit sharing can be a little devious. If you do decide to implement profit sharing with your company, it's important to be *very* transparent and open about how this is calculated. It's not a suitable option for all companies, but if it *is* suitable for yours, make sure all your company profit numbers are totally transparent so that you encourage trust within your team.

I've seen (and experienced) profit sharing which is little more than a glorified pat on the back. The idea sounds nice, but then the company has an extra profitable year and needs to pay out more than expected to the employees. The next year's profit sharing calculations tend to be adjusted down accordingly.

Bonuses calculated on personal performance are excellent incentives, and we're a fan of these in our own company. Referral bonuses are popular since it is easier to hire a new team member based upon recommendation rather than an applicant coming from who-knows-where. This can save weeks or months of time, and gives you a much higher chance of being compatible with the new team member.

For small teams or point persons on special projects, developing project bonuses can be an incentive to get specific things done quickly and efficiently. These one-off bonuses can be varied: for example, it could look like "get 300 new leads by February and we will pay out a $4,000 bonus" or it could look like "cut down email response time by 2 hours in Q3 for a $250 bonus to everyone on the team." The end goal, however structured, should be the same: help the colleagues in your company have skin in the game. Reward for effort is always a great thing for your company's long-term health.

Making It As A Remote Worker

The Importance Of Structure

If you've spent more than a few weeks working from home, you've heard multiple people making jokes about how much you are *actually* working.

What people think is irrelevant, of course, but it does point to a common problem with remote work that I've seen dozens, if not hundreds, of people struggle with.

When I worked at a regular nine-to-five office job, things were entirely different. It was highly structured. Everyone showed up to work around the same time, everyone ate lunch at around the same time, and everyone left the office around the same time. Because of this structure, traditional work does make it easy to settle into a predictable and comfortable work schedule.

I've been working remotely since 2011. Before that? I was waking up at 8, showering, driving 15 minutes to work, sitting in a fancy open plan office, grabbing coffee from the break room, going out for lunch, working until five, and heading home for dinner and a few episodes of *Buffy the Vampire Slayer* before dozing off to replicate the previous day's structure once more, groundhog style. The only variations in my daily schedule were periodic work trips, a few days in New York or Seattle, before heading straight back to the grind.

Overnight I went from this strict weekday schedule to freelancing. I had freelanced on the side previously, so the difference in the work itself wasn't challenging, but being a young adult without a normal job was a strange role to explore. At that time, there weren't really such things as coworking spaces peppered throughout every city. Most freelancers or consultants were older than I, and had stable careers which meant they probably worked from their own office rented out somewhere downtown. I was stepping into a brave new world, and the first few years were tough to deal with.

The first months were the biggest adjustment. As a freelancer, I didn't have that many pressing meetings or deadlines, so my bedtime got later, my breakfasts became brunches, and I did what most 22-year-olds do, which is drink a lot of beer at evening and drink even more coffee the next morning. I didn't have much life purpose at the time: as long as I could make rent, I considered myself doing alright. There wasn't much motivation to go the extra mile. This first few months of total freedom was enough to turn me into a potato. After this long summer of waking up at ten or eleven in the morning, staying up until three in the morning, and a lot of Pabst Blue Ribbon, I realized I needed to implement structure if I was going to do anything with my life.

I self-imposed a rigid schedule, and over the next few months things got progressively better. I began waking up at seven, showering, eating, and going to a coffeeshop to work on a very specific and tightly held schedule. I still left plenty of time for social activities (I was twenty-two, after all) but forcing an early rise was crucial to starting the day off right.

Now, before I go too far down this path, I'll have to say that I don't think the same schedule is right for everyone. I hear far too many guru hustler types talking about how they wake up at four, go to the gym, lift 500 pounds, start work by six, and make twelve sales calls by noon. These people are full of shit, so you may feel free to ignore them.

Not everyone wants to wake up at four. Or seven. Or even nine. Not everyone *needs* to go to the gym. You can do whatever you want to - but you probably do need structure.

How that structure looks like is dependent upon you, your culture, your company, your surroundings, your time zone, your career, and about one hundred other factors in your life. I can't design a perfect life for you, and neither can anyone else but yourself. The schedule itself is beside the point - because the important part is the structure, not what or when you're doing it.

The traditional corporate work structure has many downsides, not the least of which I think is a crippling inefficiency and an emphasis on quantity of work rather than quality, but there is a reason it is such a universal constant. Humans have an innate need for structure, and the enforced rigidity of a traditional work schedule creates that structure for many people who couldn't otherwise be bothered to do it for themselves.

That's why I think I need to reiterate something I've alluded to very often in this book: remote work isn't something that will work for just anyone. It works for self-directed, ambitious, disciplined people. Usually, these are people who would thrive or even exceed expectations at a normal job, so this self-direction and ambition serves them well if they decide to transition to a work-from-home or self-employed role.

One of the important things to consider about your schedule is that it shouldn't just include *work* items. It also needs to include *play* items. One of the hardest parts about working remotely is the huge social change that comes with it. You don't meet people very easily if you're holed up in your home office all the time (and video chatting with coworkers doesn't exactly count). So you've got to make sure to force yourself to get out of the house and head somewhere to have normal, face to face, human interaction. For me, that included working from a coffeeshop where I could interact with the baristas and other regulars on a daily basis. It also included heading to the local dive bar on the weekends, where I'd meet up with buddies and listen to some blues music. Whatever your jam is, it's important to schedule some real-life humanity in there along with the work, because you'll otherwise sink deep into a hole of anti-social caveman life. I've been there, done that!

Working Remotely As A Freelancer

My first job out of college was in a trendy non-profit on the East Coast, and we had the open office plan, single-origin coffee in the break room, and just about everything except fat salaries. Yet at the core, it was a much more traditionally-structured job than it appeared to be at first glance. Senior management requested their own offices (understandably) since they preferred to have telephone conversations in private and work in peace and quiet. We all showed up at 9 in the morning and left at 5 in the evening. We drove back home to eat dinner. It was quite normal.

It wasn't until a bit later that I started working remotely. After I left the trendy nonprofit job, I started freelancing. Of course, this was over a decade ago, and even in 2011 fully remote work wasn't really popular yet. Even though I worked from home or coffeeshops, the majority of my clients were still located nearby. I still had to hop on a flight from time to time and travel to an organization's headquarters or field office in order to pick up a project, but this was rare. Increasingly, though, I started gaining clients from further away, without actually meeting any key decision makers in person, and eventually a large part of my workload was entirely over the internet.

I freelanced for five years, from 2011 to 2016. Even in those five years, it was pretty impressive how the technology changed to enable remote work. In 2011, internet speeds were slower and less reliable, digital payments weren't very sophisticated, there weren't many solid places to work from, and working remotely wasn't accepted as easily as it is now.

Internet speeds were acceptable, of course, just

not amazing. Even just a few years ago, unless you were located in a large city, it was impossible to work with files over a few gigabytes in size (I did a lot of media production at the time, so large files were a big part of my work life). It would take hours to upload a rendered proof file. And given the fact that I often worked from places in Africa or Central America or Asia, I'd often leave my laptop overnight trying to upload a few hundred raw photos, only to wake up in the morning and find that the connection had died halfway through the night. Now, it seems like internet speeds are much more ubiquitously stable. Mobile internet, especially in developing countries, has grown leaps and bounds beyond what it was.

Digital payments were painful, almost nonexistent. For the first few years, I don't think I received a single digital payment. It was all checks. This is not really because the tech wasn't there (PayPal and ACH transfers were around, after all) but because large companies and nonprofit organizations were still beholden to 1990s-era payment structures, and they wouldn't use PayPal even if they had an account. It wasn't until ridiculously recently that accepting online credit card or ACH payments were made easier for freelancers or small businesses, with services like Wave or Stripe.

Working remotely was almost solely a work-from-home-office and work-from-coffeeshop thing. There were no such thing as coworking spaces, so it was Starbucks or your local third-wave coffeeshop. And most of the time, although you did tend to hobnob around with other remote workers, it felt a little bit like you were just that unemployed guy who hung out at the coffeeshop all day. Near the end of my freelance career, coworking started to become a bit of a trend. In the smaller city I was located in at the time, a single coworking space opened up, called the Hive. I went over to check it out. It was immensely depressing - basically a few folding tables stuffed into an old-school advertising company's dark back room, complete with old carpeting and musty ceiling tiles. Now, of course, coworking is a much bigger deal, but it's still not even where it could be. It's currently in a bubble of ridiculous proportions, with companies trying to rent a desk for $700 a month. Call me stingy, but $700 would buy me nine lattes per day at my local coffeeshop or an entire office of my own. At some point, I think the bubble, much like open office plans, will level out into a more moderate playing field.

The stereotype of the unemployed freelancer is still there, a little bit, but during my five years as a freelancer, people *really* didn't get it. Not having an office was equated with "unemployed" in most people's minds, as it implied I didn't have enough money to rent a space, ergo I must not be very successful, ergo I must not be very good at my job. In a way, I believe that working remotely at that point in time actually did harm my early career prospects. I don't think it's still quite the case, as people are beginning to realize that some of those shaggy hipsters nestled up in the corner of the coffeeshop are making triple the income as your typical corporate keyboard warrior. Still, the older and more traditional the industry, the more of a problem you'll find in their acceptance of remote work as a norm. If you're working in the SaaS (software-as-a-service) startup world, it's a given and people won't think twice. If you're working with toilet seat manufacturers in Alabama, well, chances are they won't really understand the concept of not having an office.

It's worth reiterating the importance of networking. Even with a more widespread acceptance of freelancing as a legitimate career, you're going to negatively affect your trajectory if you never leave your home office. Joining local communities and networking with peers is crucial to both furthering your reach now, and for years into the future.

Remote work is such a recent trend, that I don't think people often think about the long-term affects of it. It may be working fine for you right now, but think about a decade from now. Ensure that you're fostering relationships that will allow you to do the work you want to do when you are forty, fifty, or sixty years old. At that point, you might want to be in a managerial or consultant role. Is your current social and business network going to facilitate that?

Independence As A Remote Worker

Unfortunately, just because remote work is on the rise, doesn't mean it's the new normal or even that companies really know what to do with it. I've worked for remote companies, worked with dozens of remote clients, and now run a remote company, but every single one of these use cases could use improvement.

While I think the field of remote work is improving, and over the course of the past ten years there has been progress in recognizing some basic best practices in operating a distributed team, it's still got a *long* way to go. And as a worker in a remote company, you've just got to deal with these struggles as they surface.

Your level of independence is usually a direct function of how far along you are in your career.

All jobs, regardless of where they're located, give you a varying level of independence to structure your own work day. There's not really a single entry-level job, remote or not, that lets you graduate from high school or college and start defining your own work hours and responsibilities. Whether you're working in a cubicle at a multinational corporation or from the comfort of your bedroom, an entry-level employee has to endure a bit of drudgery and hunker down to do grinding work. There's usually very little room left for creativity or independence or strategizing right out of college.

However, spend a few years at work, get promoted a few times, and by the time you're in your mid thirties you can usually get a bit more flexibility in how you complete your responsibilities (and hopefully you've also gained a few more responsibilities during that time period). You probably travel for work a bit more often, are able to implement more of your own ideas into your workflow, are involved in strategy. And even in the strictest of corporate settings, you probably don't have to worry about clocking in & out like you did a few years ago.

The further you go in your career, the less your performance is gauged by how long you were warming a chair, and the more you're gauged on the actual results you've provided the company.

Why does this matter? As a remote worker, whether we like it or not, your success depends on some of the same metrics. A customer service employee is going to be gauged by the amount of calls answered, problems solved, and support cases resolved. A chief marketing officer's performance, on the other hand, is not going to be gauged by how many emails or phone calls he responds to, but by Q2's marketing ROI or last year's gross sales numbers.

All of that to say, there's only so much independence anyone can expect at first: whether you're working from home or working in an office. If you're far enough along in your career where you can have some level of control over your job role and responsibilities, things are suddenly much easier.

I think that remote work for mid-tier and upper-tier employees, or in tech-driven fields (or really anything that's new, skills-based, or disruptive) is a much easier equation to solve than remote work in entry-level, traditional fields. If you're already forging ahead in new unexplored waters, chances are there is a lot more leeway given for both management and employees. A department that hasn't changed very drastically in many years - say, for example, customer service - is much harder to deal with.

Remote work grants a large deal of independence and self-direction to colleagues who are located out of their home or coffee shops, and a good company will judge these employees by their results rather than by traditional metrics. Consider yourself fortunate if you're employed at one of these companies.

The good news about remote work really shines

if you're a freelancer. There has been a massive uptick in the amount of freelancers and consultants over the past decade, and your location independence should actually be a benefit instead of a hindrance in your career. No longer do companies find it unusual that you work from Starbucks or from your home office - it's actually quite normal.

Adjusting to remote work is easy for some people. And it's even easier if you're already the unorthodox type that bucks the trend.

I was a weird kid in college. The good thing was, I knew it. Self-awareness is important. But that doesn't change the fact that I was an incredibly nerdy dork who didn't fit in with the bros very well. and still hadn't developed the ability to grow facial hair. That didn't stop me from trying. I remember hanging out with a group and learning one of the guys was from Omaha. I cracked a joke about Warren Buffet, the oracle of Omaha, and immediately killed the room's vibe. The entire group just stared at me.

I was a bit of a misfit, clearly, but I did well in school. I worked a two or three part-time jobs while juggling a full class load, and the busyness kept me from procrastinating. I got over my initial awkwardness and networked well. Yet here's the deal: I didn't learn *anything* in *any* class. I quickly learned that the classes themselves were irrelevant: I actually didn't even have a single sit-down class with my most influential professor.

The value of college came from two things: the positive aspect of being in a closely networked private university environment, and the negative aspect of a terribly old-fashioned, expensive, and inefficient educational system. Due to the frustrations of being in a one-size-fits-all educational system I learned how to hack it, skip a lot of crap, and graduate in three years while avoiding the classes I didn't want or need. I tried to carry this lesson across into the real world: it turns out you actually *can* skip most of the stuff you don't like. You *can* hack your career.

There's no question about it: the current state of our educational system is dysfunctional. Critiquing college unequivocally across the board, however, is selling education short. Like most things, it is what you make of it. A traditional formal education seems to be more and more unnecessary for the average driven, intelligent young person. I've never once been asked about my degree, even in the multiple traditional employee positions I held right after college.

My friends from college have ended up in a wide variety of positions in life. I don't think college really influenced where they ended up: they would have gotten where they are one way or the other. I don't really even think their chosen major influenced anything, either, because certain types of people are just naturally drawn towards certain degrees. Causation rather than correlation, perhaps.

But even if I think an undergraduate degree is a good thing, in the end, it doesn't really matter. What you do with your situation - your education, your previous career, your future career, your networking - is all entirely up to you.

I suspect that my taste of college was flavored

with my particular odd slant. As I mentioned before, I didn't fit in especially well. But it was still educationally sound. I got a fairly decent academic scholarship. I couldn't have really asked for more. But because I didn't have a full scholarship, and because I felt that every semester I didn't spend in school was affecting how much I could do in actual life, I wanted to get it over with. It didn't help that I started out in graphic design, and quickly realized that unless I wanted to be perched in front of an iMac designing hospital posters for the rest of my life, I needed to get the hell out of there. So I started looking for options.

Luckily, there was a new degree track introduced by the Honors College at my university called Interdisciplinary Studies, which let students create their own major by mixing and matching classes from several disciplines. I applied and was the second student to be accepted into the new program, and I spent the next few weeks feverishly creating my own dream track and getting it approved by the provost. I scratched biology and calculus and added classes like Old & Middle English Literature, Abnormal Psychology, and Drugs, Alcohol & Crime.

Most of my professors were excited about the program and helped me draft the program. A few professors got strangely pissed off and sent me angry emails. One told me grimly "graduating early isn't in my playbook", or "I will certainly not supervise", or "there is too much at stake in skill building, ideation development and critical thinking formation to do it alone", and perhaps most impressively "you miss a lot of what creativity is about when you approach life as a check list to be completed as quickly as possible".

In the ancient world these professors operated in, there was no room for scribbling outside the lines. The possibility of having a long, lucrative career without ever going into the office was impossible to them. There wasn't much flexibility in their mindset.

I preserved these emails carefully, so I could reply after I had completed the items on my checklist as quickly as possible. I've yet to send that email, but

I plan on replying one of these days. As soon as I finish that checklist.

Often you will find managers with this same mindset: they are stuck three decades back, in a world where everyone buttoned up their suits and sent faxes. Taking a different trajectory, like working from Bali, rubs them the wrong way. Unfortunately you will have to work with these types just like anyone else, and grant them understanding even if it's not reciprocated.

Some of it just boils down to a cultural disconnect. Whether you're older or younger, an interest in remote work means you're operating on the vanguard of business. It's going to rub some folks the wrong way.

Finding A Remote Job

We've covered some of the fundamentals of how managers can find remote employees, but how does an employee find a remote job? It's not as simple as reversing the process, unfortunately.

The hard part about getting a remote job is not the availability or lack of volume, of course - there are hundreds of remote jobs opening up every day, and they're becoming available in more and more industries. The trick is about getting noticed, and making sure you stand out among the hundreds of other applicants...because you won't find a more competitive application process anywhere outside of

Silicon Valley itself.

It's probably useful to give a behind-the-scenes look at the hiring process that remote companies use. You'll quickly see that the key to success in getting a remote role is to set yourself apart from the other applicants, and getting a conversation going with someone at your target company.

When we post a job opening at Discosloth, we don't just get a few dozen good applications. We get *hundreds* in the first few weeks. Remote job opportunities are so in demand that our job postings automatically get scraped and syndicated across the web to twenty or thirty remote job boards, and after a few months we can get over a thousand applicants even for a niche position.

Just like we have a handful of important criteria that every applicant needs to fulfill, every other company out there is also looking for a specific person who is perfect for their role. For an entry-level Google Ads specialist, for example, we want to know that the applicant fits with Discosloth's vibe, has a well-defined hard skillset, can work well remotely, and fits our salary requirements.

Are there a thousand quality applicants in the world who fulfill our requirements? Perhaps, but out of our group of thousand applicants, we can filter them pretty quickly. It's a little disappointing, but I can usually glance across a resume or CV and automatically filter out 90% of the applicants within seconds simply because they don't have the requisite skillset.

And that's Lesson 1: apply only for relevant opportunities. The shotgun approach does *not* work well for remote roles. This means that each application process will be a little more time intensive and selective, but spending extra time on personalizing your resume and communication for each open role will probably serve you better than spending time on applying to just any random remote role that you see opening up.

Now that I've gotten our field of applicants narrowed down to a hundred or so, after looking at their skills, I then look at their experience. I'll be upfront: work experience doesn't really matter that much to me. But life experiences *do* matter, and they're especially relevant in a remote role. Some of the best applications I've seen include details on their life experiences like hobbies, interests, and especially travel. Taking a summer off to travel Asia, or spending a few months in college working in a ski resort, or running half marathons, producing short films for your local film festival, working in foreign countries - all of those are things that indicate you're creative, daring, take risks, and can probably handle working from a distance.

And that's Lesson 2: be personal and share your experiences. Emphasize travel, personal independence, and entrepreneurial pursuits.

After looking for candidates who have included their personal experiences, I'm probably left with thirty or forty solid resumes that tell a good story. I usually have a hunch that all of these applicants would fit with Discosloth's vibe. This leaves me with the boring but essential task of reaching out to every one of these possible applicants and doing a little back-and-forth before inviting them to a preliminary interview.

That's Lesson 3: Be prompt and reachable. You'd think that all of these applicants would be interested in a job, right? Wrong. The number one reason that we pick someone else for an interview is because they actually responded promptly. A surprising number of applicants simply don't get back to me, or if they do it's four days after I sent them an email. There is no excuse for this, because every company is using this response time as a gauge to see how engaged and punctual the applicant is. If you can't even get back to a company quickly after they reach out to you, that's a major red flag.

I'm probably left with 5-10 decent applicants at this point - punctual, qualified, and interested. Ideally I'll be able to have a video interview with all of these applicants, but realistically something comes up in the back-and-forth that makes either the applicant or myself realize we're not a good fit. Salary, expectations, communication style, or simply not a great vibe.

As an applicant, I'd make it my priority to get

into that last round of video interviews. This is the most important of all sections of the job application process, and *the first video interview makes or breaks a hire*. Make yourself stand out, apply to highly relevant positions, make your resume tell a personal story rather than a collection of GPA scores and college classes, and be professional and responsive to inquiries from the company.

Remember that you're applying for one of the most competitive types of positions ever, and you're competing with people from every location in the entire world. Used to be, you're competing with others in your city. With remote work, you now live in a city of billions.

Personal Downsides of Remote Work

When something new appears on the horizon, the excitement in the air is palpable. You start seeing the tweets, overhearing buzzwords in conversation, and inevitably some community bloggers on Forbes start publishing those articles about 5 ways to make your AI-powered chatbot drive ten times revenue for your influencer marketing business.

The same happened with remote work. The internet got faster, and suddenly remote work exploded. Why work from the office if I can work from home? Why work from home if I can work from the beach?

I've been working remotely for a while now, so I can't really blame anyone who's on board the same ship I am. It's a quite nice ship. I've seen forty-odd countries from the deck of this ship.

However, if we take a look at the life cycle of other work related trends, you'll see a pattern develop. First it's the hype. Then it's the implementation. Then it's the reality.

For a long time open-plan offices were hyped to us as a perk - work in the same large airy, echoey space as your CEO! - and it was, admittedly, pretty cool. But at the same time it was an incredibly unpractical and sometimes painful setup to work in. An entry-level employee like me didn't really need to hear the CEO argue on speakerphone all day.

Over the past decade (man, doesn't time fly?) of working remotely I have come to realize that remote work might not be the magic bullet we first thought it was. I still *love* remote work, but there are a plethora of problems and downsides that need to be honestly faced before you can make it work for yourself or for your company.

As Discosloth has grown we have hired on remote employees, both full-time and part-time. It's
been a learning experience. Thankfully, I think digital marketing is one of the most applicable fields for
remote workers. All of our time is spent on the internet anyway. But I actually am not sure we will
always be 100% remote. I could visualize us transitioning into a traditional office sooner than later, if
only for the luxury of having a coffeemaker, water
cooler, printer, and the ability to separate my work
life from everyday life.

I've worked remotely as a freelancer, as an employee, and as a boss. The dynamics are different in
all three roles, but the reality is that you can't treat it
the same as a normal job. I was curious how others
feel about the downsides of remote work. I know
I'm weird, and my problems probably aren't everyone's problems. Thankfully I've got an expansive
network of folks working remotely, and many of
them were able to join in with their thoughts.

Timothy Jensen is a PPC marketer, and works
remotely just like we do at Discosloth. He said that

the "biggest downside can be maintaining boundaries between personal and work life. Particularly in a house with small kids, it's important to have a separate space for an office (for me, it's the basement) and clear boundaries for when I'm at work and not available."

We don't have kids in the house right now, but I can see that being a game changer.

I met Holly Ragsdale around the same time I started working remotely, at a little coffeeshop outside the college we both attended. She now works remotely as a content lead for Booj Digital. Her response was similar. She says the hardest part about remote work is losing human contact. "But I remedy that with at least 1–2 coffee shop visits a week," she says. "Breaking up the week by being in a social setting has helped me tremendously. I'm also spoiled in the fact that my husband works from home (as a programmer) about 80% of the time, so I don't get as lonely as I would if he had a more traditional office job. Having a dog and taking lots of walks helps too!"

Michael Bogosian runs Blacksmith Digital, an internet marketing company. He says "I'd say the biggest downside to remotely working is the opportunity to connect with other people and ride the wave of creativity that's often produced in a group setting. Video conferencing does wonders to bridge the gap in many situations but nothing beats a power workshop in person with your client/resource. The energy and satisfaction can be palpable. I just don't get that from video, email, chat, sms, or phone."

I tend to agree with Michael. As much as software companies like to tout their messaging and project management solutions for improving remote communication, sometimes it's just not enough.

Jordan Ayres says "For me, there are no downsides. With that said, I have friends and colleagues who mention that they miss being around people. It's also worth mentioning that I split my time between an office and working remotely, so I'm not fully remote. Although this would be my preferred work arrangement. But for anyone who feels this downside, it's important to socialize outside of work. I make sure I have fun stuff to do in the evening that involves spending time with real people and not behind a screen, whether that's going to an improv class, jiu-jitsu, or even going for a drink with a friend. I'd much rather spend less time socializing at work and more time socializing outside of work."

I then posed an either/or question to everybody. If they had to pick between remote work or not remote work for the rest of their life, which would they pick?

Timothy Jensen says "At this point, I would say I would pick remote. I worked in an open office setting in the past, and while there are positives in being face to face with people you're working with, the negatives of the distracting environment outweigh the positives for getting work done. In the digital marketing industry, it's just frankly not necessary to be in the same room all the time."

Michael Bogosian says "I've settled into an office lately where I can close my door and have some privacy. As a new parent, working from home just doesn't work anymore. I still run my business with all my resources and clients remotely. I just rely on one a central location to set up shop more than I used to."

I asked Jordan, who worked a few days a week from home, if he noticed any difference in the amount or type of work he gets done. "Yes. When I'm at home, I'm more productive and the quality of my work improves. This is because it's much harder to be distracted and it uses up less willpower and mental energy. As I mentioned above, when I want to focus on a task, I shut down all distractions. It's easier to do this when working from home."

Holly said the same. "I would absolutely choose remote work. In today's world, so much (and arguably everything in the tech/writing/communication world) can be done through the use of technology, so working from anywhere makes so much sense to me. I also know that I can handle working remotely after these two years, so I feel confident that I could sustain it long-term." She also says that she sticks to a 9-5 in Central Time while her team does 9–5 in Mountain Time. "We are only an hour off so it hasn't affected us too much. I do love being an hour ahead of them because I feel like I've accomplished so much by the time they sign on, and I just love that feeling of being ahead and on top of things (rather than behind and catching up as soon as I start work). All of our clients are in different time zones (one of mine is Pacific and the other is Eastern), so it's a lot to keep track of but it makes things interesting. I do think keeping specific hours is helpful, so you don't feel like your schedule for the day is unknown. It helps set a healthy boundary between work and home life; when 5:00 hits, I do a good job of walking away from my computer."

We've all had one of those jobs - the demanding, micromanaged, cog-in-a-machine grinding sort that consumes your life inside the office and out.

Work/life balance is a popular topic these days, and you'll see lots of posts getting shared on LinkedIn about burnout, treating yourself right, not checking your email after five o'clock, and similar things.

Remote work puts a further layer of complication on the subject. Because remote workers so often work from home, it's much more difficult to turn off your work: especially if you're across the world from the rest of your team.

It's a bit easier when you're essentially in the same time zone as the rest of your team, but when the entire team is scattered between Bali, California, Spain, and Russia, things start looking differently. Compromise is required.

With the freedom and independence that remote work gives you, much can be required: and this means you can't hold strictly to traditional work hours. Flexibility is important, even if it means not working in the morning, but having to work later into the evening.

This makes it difficult, at times, to turn work off. How much you disconnect yourself from work is a personal choice, and depends upon how dedicated you are to advancing a career. Personal priorities and a multitude of additional environmental factors play into this. Are you about to retire? Don't worry about breaking your back. Do you desperately need a raise or a promotion? Might be worth the extra hours.

I've found that creating separation in your physical environment is one of the easiest ways to mentally encapsulate your work.

Having a home office (not just a desk in your bedroom, or a spot at the kitchen table) was one of the most important things that helped me to clearly define work time from non-work time. I can go into the office and shut the door, sit down in my office chair, and know that I'm at work.

If you don't do this, it's easy to be sitting on the couch during the weekend, the same place where you often work, and drift into sending some emails and looking over the accounting. Just like it's equally easy to crash on the couch during work, and drift off into researching cool weekend trips on the internet, or watching a YouTube video.

If you're a traveling nomad (as I was for years) then it gets a bit harder to create this physical separation. You can rarely find the perfect Airbnb that includes a home office. My solution to this is to go to coffeeshops to work - even a few hours of focused work is usually enough for me to get the vast majority of daily projects done.

Sometimes, work just follows you around anyway, and to a degree this is entirely okay.

Think about it from a broader perspective. If you had a traditional office job, you'd be gone from eight in the morning to six in the evening. You'd waste a lot of time commuting, burn a lot of time goofing off at the desk, and take an hour or more for lunch. It's not terribly efficient.

Working from home, or from the road, frees up hours and hours of your time. Perhaps you can't divorce yourself from work as easily as going home from a traditional office, but the upside is: you're traveling. You're in Bali. Maybe having to work evenings isn't so bad, after all?

Remote Workflow & Communication

When Process Gets In The Way Of Progress

Process in business is important. Process, when you boil it down to the most crucial element, is the science of *making things happen*. But the instant that process suddenly gets in between your people and the goal, and *stops* things from happening, is the instant that process is your enemy.

Different processes work for different businesses. Some businesses need next to no process. For example, a yoga studio just requires that people show up, pay, sit for a class, and leave. At best you'll need a schedule, payroll, and a few bills each month that need to be paid. An automobile factory, on the other hand, has millions of intertwining processes that must be matched together like clockwork. The two aren't even comparable.

Remote work is *not* for the majority of companies. If you're one of the 3.8 million retail businesses in the United States employing 42 million workers, you cannot work remotely. You've got a physical brick and mortar store which requires people to show up to every morning. The same with restaurants (15 million workers) or factories (13 million workers). You simply can't manufacture an automobile from a distance, and that's why most traditional business wisdom doesn't apply to remote work.

Companies that can successfully hire remote workers are focused in a few very specific niches: services (engineering, law, architecture), software (development and IT), creative (design, writing, multimedia) and internet (ecommerce, publishing, marketing). Often even larger physically based companies can incorporate remote work into their workflow (for example, a manufacturer can turn their marketing department into a remote team) but this ultimately requires the remote team to follow the same processes as the physically based company.

That's why the processes that have been working for decades for traditional companies don't often work well for remote teams.

A few years ago I worked with a colleague who was *obsessed* with process. As part of the marketing team taking charge of the content marketing strategy, he would create elaborate spreadsheets carefully defining schedules, painstakingly analyzing keyword lists, creating rubrics that assigned efficacy scores to different concepts, detailing the titles of each and every blog post, segmenting audiences into hyper-specific demographics, and so on.

Now, even ignoring the conversation on how smart these tactics are anyway in today's marketing world, this colleague was missing a major point in dealing with a remote team.

We happened to have a pretty fantastic remote team. We had a solid analytics lead, a web developer,

and a content lead who worked extremely well together. Even though we were in three entirely separate locations, each time we got together, we could
brainstorm ideas, create them, and then implement
them in a matter of days or weeks. Our metrics were
fantastic, and the numbers just kept getting better.
We were doing solid work that we were proud of.

The key to our team's success was personality.
We worked well together (congeniality is incredibly
important) but we were also individually highly independent, and could structure our days and priorities with little oversight or input from others. We
liked to work with each other, but we were still able
to get most of our work done without too much micromanagement or detailed guidance. In short, the
perfect remote team.

When this colleague started bringing in a workflow that he had become used to in his previous traditional corporate job, he suddenly threw a wrench
into the works. The process was so onerous to a team
of free-thinking, independent workers that it killed
the creativity and spontaneous thinking that had

guided our work so far. Instead of a balanced and respectful brainstorming session in which we would listen to the feedback from team members and reach a common ground, we were instead forced into a rigid workflow.

This colleague was a fan of agile methodology. Now, there are tomes of thought already written about agile workflow, enough that it's hardly worth revisiting, but he imposed a structure on top of an already functional team that essentially broke our productivity. As the newly dubbed "sprint leader" he imposed spreadsheets that documented everything, began scheduling too many meetings to match with the phases of the sprint, and essentially overrode our existing flattened hierarchy a top-down hierarchy that didn't need to be there. Projects that would take a month to complete were either condensed into two-week lengths or cut completely. Projects that couldn't just fit into an Excel template with a voting list of pros and cons were put to the side. Our time spent in communicating things doubled, and our actual output halved.

This colleague's error was in two assumptions.

First, he made the mistaken assumption that all people work the same. He assumed that since this process had worked somewhere else in the past, it would work here as well. He did not realize that there are many different types of personalities, and some of them don't require close task management.

Second, he made the error in thinking that micromanagement works in a remote team. He failed to realize that the best remote teams actually need the *least* direct management: after all, they are working by themselves, quite literally. They have no manager looking over their shoulders. They have no standardized work hours. They are probably some of the most independent employees on the planet, and they will *always* do better when they can take responsibility for their own output and decisions.

Creating good processes for remote teams means that you've got to understand your team, and the way they work, before anything else.

Now, you can either create the process and hire people for that process, or you can hire people and create the process for them. One is going to be easier than the other depending on your situation.

Since I believe good people are harder to find than processes, my personal preferences is for creating a process for the team, not a team for the process.

Because ultimately (and this is in direct conflict with the advice suggested in many business management books) the end question is whether things get done. The process of just how it is done is totally irrelevant, and the more time you spend on the *how* means you're not doing the actual *it*.

That's why I suggest hiring with your end goal in mind. You want to have a remote team? Hire someone who works well remotely, and that will always be someone who works well without oversight and micromanagement. You want X done? Your employee already works well without oversight, so the process required to get X done should be as hands-free, time-efficient, and independent as possible.

Jordan Ayres, whose thoughts I shared in a previous chapter, works several days a week from home, balanced by a few days spent at the office. I asked him how his company manages remote work and institutes processes for better productivity and efficiency.

"The fundamental philosophy," Jordan says, "that works for my paid media team, is to create and use software, systems and processes that free up our time and energy to focus on what clients pay us to do: improve their performance. For example, our acquisition team is split into two. There are both account managers and executives. The account manager's handle client communication while the executives manage the client's paid accounts. This means that most of the time, as an executive, I can focus on shutting down all distractions and working on the account. I'll only check my email, Slack, or Asana if I need more information/have questions about the client's business. I've found the key to fostering communication and productive work is as follows. First, minimize distractions. Second, create processes, checklists and systems. Third, schedule time for "deep work". Fourth, schedule internal meetings and admin work when you have the least amount of energy and creative output (mine is in the afternoon). And finally, focus on urgent and important tasks first."

I asked the same question of Timothy Jenson. His company uses a mixture of tools for communication, using Skype for both group and individual chats. They keep an orderly approach to document organization. "In general," Timothy says, "being available and responsive during normal work hours is exceptionally important when working remote (while at the same time respecting boundaries of personal time)."

Michael Bogosian has been working remotely full-time for over eight years. "Communication has changed throughout my career. It used to be exclusively through email, text, chat, and phone calls in the beginning. I relied heavily on Google's G-suite products and basic management tools like calendar events. Now, we've progressed into an age where I have 3-4 places I have to check to respond to messages like Slack, Google Hangouts, LinkedIn, Up-

Work, Fiverr, etc. It's a little ridiculous. Slack's use of channels makes interdepartmental communications easier. It also allows me to set up groups for specifics projects, which I like. I'm very pleased with how G-suite has grown up. Google Drive has become incredibly robust and interconnected. All the products work well together and foster a great amount of collaboration among remote teams. My general philosophy around communication is to keep it light. I am acutely aware of the lack of human connection with respect to body language conveyed via chat or SMS. If there is a topic that requires me to truly understand how someone feels about a strategy or approach I prefer a video conference, or at minimum a phone call. I try and use chat or SMS for tactical communications. Same goes for my email. I tend to use email as a log of what was discussed as opposed to a place where I develop a strategy."

A few years ago, I worked at a remote company that tried hard at improving their process flow. They had not always been a remote company, which means they had inherited a long ancestry of traditional, corporate workflow that had morphed into a remote workflow.

Unfortunately, the company was just large enough that the workflow had become fairly awkward. When you go remote, you suddenly run into a lot of new problems, chief of which is communication. The power of watercooler talk is really underrated, and it turns out that when you go remote, watercooler talk is eliminated.

I'm sure HR departments everywhere would love that idea, but in reality it has a huge negative effect on company communications. There is such a strong power in nonverbal communication that immediately stops when a company goes remote, that there's no effective way to communicate urgency or goals in the same manner. Not only do employees get left in the dark about important company movements, but managers are clueless as to the small things that affect a team's morale.

In an effort to increase the camaraderie and

communication between teams, the company instituted a few platforms that were to ostensibly help
stop this gap. The company used OKR tools (to
measure objectives and key results), NPS polls (to
measure net promotor score), peer recognition (virtual high fives), Slack channels, coaching, and platforms that helped institute continuous feedback.

The problem is that among the half-dozen new
platforms each employee had to adopt, each ate up
hours of time each week, was easily gameable, felt
artificial and corporate, and ultimately fractured the
attention and emotions of everyone. Because, after
all, no one decides to work at a remote company
because they wanted a *more* corporate environment.

What would have worked in this company?
Many things, perhaps but what it was actually missing was a simple hierarchical structure with a quarterly performance meeting - you know, the sort of
simple process that has been in place for decades.
And since this company was moderately sized, it was
also lacking a regular alternative for watercooler sessions. In short, there was no unstructured time for

employees to meet others in the company, chat about goals, discover what other people are doing, or just brainstorm ways to be better at their jobs.

Too much process can kill the spirit of a company. A crucial part of relationships, both professionally and socially, involve conversation and casual chit-chat. When you have less personal interaction anyway in a remote company, dumping even more process into the problem just exacerbates the issue.

Removing Time From Productivity

We've all had one of those jobs - the demanding, micromanaged, cog-in-a-machine sort that consumes your life inside the office and out.

Part of this is just the expected and normal career path: right out of school, entry level workers have to sludge through less-than-desirable positions until they're promoted into a role that doesn't require detailed management of work hours. Another part of this is a systematically broken approach to productivity. It changes entirely once remote work is brought into the picture.

We still see this antiquated sort of vantage point,

every once in a while, when we bring on a consulting client for our agency. We are results-focused rather than process-focused, and we don't charge by the hour. Since we're a vendor, not an employee, we charge a flat retainer fee and deliver the results accordingly.

I think it's a pretty simple model (you pay us, we give you something) but from time to time we've had clients confused about our approach.

Some time ago, a long-term client switched up their internal roles and a new point person was assigned to our account. Although we had been nailing all of the performance metrics for this particular client since the beginning - improving on cost and volume goals every single month - this new director of marketing didn't seem to understand the concept of results-focused work, rather than a corporate process. Almost immediately she began demanding a smorgasbord of information: accounting for all the hours we were spending on the project, weekly meetings to discuss strategies, using her new task board instead of our internal scheduling, sending countless emails, and worst of all, totally revamping our own strategies.

We began spending so much time on red tape that the actual project began suffering. Although we tried to work with her on the communication process, it was clear she wasn't interested in negotiating. I was confused of her reasoning for weeks, until she shared her screen one day and accidentally left her Notes app visible: a personal laundry list of complaints about our company.

We realized that she was upset that Discosloth wasn't working forty hours a week on her project... yet each month we charged over double what she made.

Yet, our marketing consulting was directly responsible for over 60% of the company's revenue. We'd doubled their leads over the previous five months and added hundreds of thousands of dollars of revenue. How we tracked our time, processes, and strategies was irrelevant, but she didn't seem to feel the same way.

Of course, this example isn't a standard employee-employer scenario, but I think it reflects the same sort of mentality pervasive in the corporate world: a focus on *time* rather than *productivity*. Just like an ineffective employee can generate a paperwork trail and appear highly productive, a systemic focus on tracking hours can also be a facade that hides actual productivity.

When you're working with a remote team, all of the time-based productivity problems inherent in a traditional office are multiplied by ten. There are many rules and guidelines that are negotiable with remote work, but flexible working hours is not one of them.

Giving your team the ability and flexibility to work whenever they want, on their own time, is one of the most important things you can do for both their success and yours. Here's why.

First, people who are going into remote roles are looking for increased flexibility. Otherwise, they'd be commuting into a normal job. Being locked down to a certain range of working hours makes absolutely no sense for the remote worker. For starters, this ties them down to a specific time zone. If you're based on the East Coast and require a typical nine-to-five working day, these inflexible working hours make it almost impossible for someone to work anywhere else than Eastern Standard or Central time. What use is it to have a remote job if you can't move to Pacific time if you want to? You'll be required to work from 6am to 2pm every day. Working from London would require an employee to clock in from 2pm to 10pm every day. Neither of which is an ideal schedule for everyone.

Second, having hourly-based expectations for your team is priming you for disappointment (unless you're running a customer support team or call center, of course). Remote work already requires a significant amount of trust and independence in both the team and the individual employee. You are, hopefully, already employing independent and ambitious high-performers. Forcing these high-performers to accommodate arbitrary working hours is going to backfire. They should already know what sort of schedule works for them personally, and it's better to let them decide how they are most productive.

Third, if you've got employees in different time zones, they're likely in different cultures as well, none of which operate on the same schedule as yours. Hiring an Italian is an excellent idea, but you shouldn't expect them to be available at two in the afternoon, because that is when every single Italian in the entire country has popped down to the cafe for an espresso. Hiring a Russian is also an excellent idea, but expecting them to break for lunch at noon is bizarre: it's actually eaten closer to three or four.

Time does not equal productivity. There's a lot of research out there on the subject, but like most research it always seems to conflict with each other. Companies are not factories (well, unless they *are* factories, of course). Unless your tasks are insanely menial, employees should be expected to ebb and flow in their productivity. Think about your own level of productivity throughout the day, or even throughout the week. Do you sit down at your desk at 9am on Monday and start churning out a consistent level of work until 5pm on Friday?

Of course not. Everyone's pattern of output varies. In general, I'd say mine starts with a burst of productivity on Monday, getting back into the flow of business, answering emails, starting small projects for the week. I might get a little bogged down with work during the middle of the week, going at a slower pace. Near the end of the week I usually get a fresh burst, getting some stuff done before Friday. Halfway through Friday, I'm wiped out, and it's time to crack open a cold one around lunchtime. I pick up the laptop a few times during the weekend to get caught up on stuff that's still happening and respond to any urgent emails. And then the entire cycle happens over again.

Each day is even more granular. I love to get up early and get the most urgent stuff out of the way, freeing up my time later in the day for creative work (the part of our business that I really enjoy). There are significant dead times in the middle of the day where I don't get a lot done - we take a long lunch, and usually there is an hour or so mid-afternoon when I'm running errands or taking a walk or doing something else that requires daylight hours. Sometimes I work late into the night, other times I've retired to the garage, fiddling with things by four in the afternoon.

How many hours do I work during the week? Honestly, I'm not really sure. Some weeks it could be twenty hours. Others it might be sixty. It's irrelevant. I get things done when they need to be done. If nothing needs to be done, I'm not under any pressure to do anything.

This mindset isn't terribly structured, but in the context of a remote company, it's essential. You're already working in locations scattered across the world: why not work in all sorts of time periods, as well?

There are downsides that come with this approach, as well, so it's important to analyze those. Here's some of the reasons why this unstructured approach can be tough to implement.

First, some companies and verticals require more

in-person communication than others. Whether that's a phone call or a video call, this means that, at a minimum, some level of overlap might be required. Most companies work with this by establishing a minimal amount of required working hours: for example, one of the past companies I worked at required all employees worldwide to be able to work from 8am to 10am Pacific Time. This was actually a quite important rule for this company, allowing teams located anywhere in the world to be able to interface with each other without too much focus on if a particular person would be available. It was general knowledge that *everyone* would be available for those two hours during the day, and this fact was known up front before joining the company. Whenever I was in Central Time, I'd be available from 10am to noon. Whenever I was in Europe, I'd just shift that ahead a few hours so that I was always available between 6pm to 8pm. We have a similar rule at Discosloth, although we're a bit more flexible about it.

Second, some roles and industries are still based

MAKING REMOTE WORK WORK

on hours. I think we're all slowly evolving towards a better and more results-focused mentality. Yet, you'll find some backlash from people set in the old ways of calculating worth based on hours. Software developers still have a strange knack of calculating their salary based upon hours rather than value added to the company. Even if they end up making the same amount of money at the end of the year (or more!) it can be difficult to shift their approach from being paid on a time-spent basis to being paid on a holistic results basis.

Triaging Communication

When you transition your team to asynchronous communication, you'll find that your communication process changes drastically. But it shouldn't be too complicated: on the other hand, it actually becomes significantly simplified.

Although we would love for these sorts of things to work themselves out naturally (and they often do especially for very small teams) the reality is that, for a remote team, some standards need to be set for how to approach communication.

At previous companies I've worked at, there was not really a standard company-wide policy (or set of guidelines) that helped people decide *how* to communicate. The result was an often cluttered and inefficient circle of communication that got more complicated the more people were involved. One person might send an email about an urgent subject, and get upset that nothing was done about it by the following morning. Another person who loved talking face-to-face might call a video meeting for something that actually didn't need to happen for another month or so. Priorities would swiftly get out of whack, because employees (out of good faith, to be fair) would focus on whatever was communicated in the most urgent fashion, rather than what was *actually* urgent.

At Discosloth, we automatically avoid most of these big communication issues by having small teams, but in order to scale we have a triage system. It's quite simple.

Non-urgent tasks that need to be done eventually? That's best done with an email. As is usual in the business world, an email is expected to be answered within one business day.

Moderately urgent tasks that need to be done now, but probably not life-changing? That's best done with a chat message. It's also a good way to have a discussion about something technical. Email is too back-and-forth for technical problems, yet you usually need a paper trail to reference, which means that a phone call can be difficult.

Urgent things that require immediate attention? These are best communicated via a phone call or a video meeting. It's also the best way to talk about anything financially or personally sensitive - or whenever something might involve heightened emotions.

I've floated our strategy around to various individuals who work in wildly different industries and roles. I've not received unanimous agreement on my approach, which tells me that different strokes work for different folks. Specifically, speaking with a team lead at a software development company, I learned that he absolutely *hated* email, and the rest of his team did as well. Digging deeper into the reasons why, it surfaced that their company used email tickets for bug requests and support issues. Furthermore, the company decided to implement communication based solely on Jira (a software planning service from Atlassian that is focused towards software companies using an agile methodology). This software development company even required their customers to sign up with a Jira account in order to communicate with them.

I can identify a multitude of things wrong with this approach, but the most prominent seems to be the blanket aversion to email and the requirement that clients adopt Jira. This makes sense for developers, but not for the real world, in which customers aren't always tech-focused (if they were, they wouldn't be calling *you*, would they?) and definitely don't know how to use Jira effectively. It's worth taking a step backwards to analyze just what's happening with communication. The team despised email, and rightfully so - as they used it, they were having to keep track of countless issues, bugs, and feature changes through email, a clunky medium for constant feedback loops.

I consider that a total misuse of email. Unless you're discussing a new feature in a high-level, abstracted way, I wouldn't ever recommend using email when a team is trying to figure out software bugs. Triaging this in our manner would instead mean that the issue is best solved asynchronously (likely via chat) or a ticketing system.

That is what drove them to adopt Jira. So far, so good. They recognized email wasn't working for bug requests, so they moved to something a little more suited for that. The error, however, comes when they require all of their clients to also use the platform. That might sound ideal, but this is a classic communication disconnect between developers and customers. Developers don't usually relish the idea of talking to anyone, especially clients. Software people communicate *far differently* than non-software people. Usually, between each other a group of developers will do pretty well in conveying all the appropriate information, but throw an outsider into the mix and it goes haywire. Shifting communication platforms will not solve anything when you have an underlying fundamental communication flaw, and expecting your clients to use Slack or Jira in a manner that meshes with your internal development flow is a further mistake.

The solution to this would be to put a communicator in between the developer and the client, which is usually a good idea anyway. It's a rare developer who enjoys, or is good at, talking with the uninitiated. Too many frustrations exist when one party of the conversation doesn't understand fundamental tech-speak, and the other party doesn't understand fundamental business-speak. Depending on the organization, that buffer might be a project manager, a C-level officer, a sales executive, or a team lead.

There are some things you cannot change, and one of those things is external communication. Anyone who's ever had a client knows that they're the boss, whether we like it or not, and the likelihood of training them on a specific manner of communication is slim to none. They're paying us, after all, so part of our work is communicating with them. It's up to us to adopt to their standard, not vice versa.

When we triage communication - three different tiers of issues which are split between email, chat, and direct communication - we use this internally, but not necessarily externally. A crucial element of our entire existence as a company means that we make it easier, not harder, for our customers to communicate what they need. Therefore, we bend to their needs and adjust communication accordingly.

Some of our clients love email. Some of our clients prefer chat. Some of our clients love the telephone. We have a point person within the company designated as the primary contact for each client, and we serve as the mediator (the "account executive" for lack of a better word) and translate the client's communication into whichever internal medium works best for the issue, so the rest of the company knows what's going on, as well as the relative urgency of the issue.

Remote Technologies

It seems like every year brings another iteration of software that promises to revolutionize the way businesses communicate. Slack, HipChat, Hang-outs, Trello, Asana, Superhuman, the list goes on eternally.

I once worked in a tool-obsessed company. We had a tool for *everything*, and because the company was also a bit corporate and overly obsessed with metrics, there was a lot of everything. There was a tool to track company, departmental, and personal KPIs (key performance indicators). There was a tool to track NPS (net promoter score, which is a form of gauging customer satisfaction). There was a tool to track time off. There was a tool to track employee happiness. There was a tool to collect anonymous employee sentiment and suggestions. There was an app for the annual Secret Santa. At one point they were even toying with the idea of adopting an app that encouraged employees to pay attention to their physical health.

On top of that, add hundreds of spreadsheets and Trello and emails and Hangouts and Slack and a custom CRM and Zoom, and then again a few *more* specialized tools for each department. Simply on-boarding a new employee took months, and even then it was a constant struggle to remember how to properly use all of these tools in the course of an average workday.

Some level of tooling is critical to a company's continued success, especially as it scales. But I'm a big believer in minimizing the amount of tools used in the process. If it doesn't make you *more* money and time, it's making you *lose* money and time.

The level of tooling at this particular company

was perhaps more suited to a company of 5,000 rather than a company of 50, which will always have a lower revenue, a greater margin of error, and more dependence upon personal responsibility and productivity.

For most companies who are exploring the possibility of remote work, ideally you are a small and adaptive group of workers. Simplicity is key. And more than anything, quality communication is key.

In the end, you just need three forms of communication: visual, auditory, and literary. People need to transfer words to other people. Just how those words are communicated is mostly irrelevant, as long as they arrive at the intended recipient and are responded to as needed.

Although it's always a good idea to search for tools and processes that speed up communication, cut down misunderstandings, and improve efficiency, you must always remember that *new tools don't fix poor communication*. If anything, adding new tools into the mix makes poor communication even worse. Get your organization talking together in a productive manner first, and *then* add the tools.

If your company is having problems communicating over phone and email, then the problems are not in the mode of communication: the problem lies in your company. Millions of companies have effectively used email and phone to communicate for decades. Adding Slack or HipChat or Trello to the mix will not fix your problems.

My pessimistic viewpoint on the importance of tools has been often challenged by others in the startup space, and it's good to listen to them as well. I'm not always right (some would say I'm not always *wrong*) and my opinion is just one of billions on earth.

However, I like gadgets as much as the next nerd, and over the years we have structured a workflow that works well for smaller remote companies. It's not very glamorous, but it's simple and effective. There's a straightforward rubric for success when you're adopting processes and tools for communicating in a small remote company.

My guidelines are: keep the cost per user down, keep barriers to adoption low, minimize the ongoing time required by the tool, encourage *quality* interaction rather than *quantity*, and perhaps most important to cap the amount of communication platforms to a total of three or four.

Keeping the cost per user low is important, especially when considering the cost of scaling. It may seem trivial to adopt a few platforms which cost $10-30 per month for a seat. However, imagine a company in which twenty users are on six or seven platforms each (it sounds excessive, but I've seen companies with more). Suddenly your small company is paying $25,000 a year for monthly subscriptions that are actually making communication worse. If your company scales to include fifty or sixty employees, you're suddenly paying as much for the privilege of fancy spreadsheet apps as for an entire full-time office manager position, which might be a more effective usage of your budget.

Barriers to adoption are also important to consider. Tools only work well if everybody is using them, otherwise you'll soon discover that some team members will be out of the loop without even knowing it, simply because they didn't see the message posted in the quarterly goals app a few weeks ago. And that means everyone ends up resorting to email anyway, to pass along the same information.

Ongoing investment of time is one of the least considered, but perhaps most costly of all, aspects of adopting tools. If each user spends just ten minutes a day per platform, extrapolate for the whole year. Suddenly each platform takes 41 hours a year, or *an entire week of productivity loss*. Does each platform, in turn, provide your company with over a week of value per user?

Encouraging quality of communication over quantity of communication is also vastly important. Which is more succinct and accurate: a detailed yet brief email, or an endless group chat? Of course, different approaches for different beasts, but if we sit down and analyze various methods of discussion I can rarely see the benefit of a free-for-all, sentence-by-sentence chat-storm approach to discussing a problem, rather than a measured and slowly paced email exchange. Or better yet, a simple phone call or video meeting.

And finally, capping the sheer number of implemented communication platforms is probably a very good strategy for smaller companies to keep in mind. Accommodate the written word (emails for bigger issues, chat for immediate non-intrusive communication) and the spoken word (phone calls or video calls). You really shouldn't need more than three or four platforms. For example, within Discosloth we use internal email, Google Chat, Zoom, and Google Calendar - that is all that we need, and adding another platform into the mix would just fragment things more.

Best Practices For Managing Employees Remotely

Most of us with a few years of work under our belt have had similar experiences, but I've experienced the entire gamut of fantastic managers and terrible managers. Likewise, if we polled everyone who has ever worked under me, I think we'd have a similar range of opinions that range from painting me in an angelic to an absolutely demonic light.

At this point, I've worked more years remotely than I've worked in a physical office. The dynamic is different, but it's work all the same. And the more I work with people, whether as a client or a vendor or a boss, the more I suspect that being a good remote manager isn't that hard.

Acting in good faith, being diligent, paying attention to detail, and working hard to interact with your employees on a personal basis is all that is required to turn a dysfunctional remote team into a well-oiled machine. That's right: exactly the same sort of soft skills that is required to make a traditional team located in a central office work well together. Unfortunately, as we all know, it seems like those soft skills are a little hard to find. Remote or not.

A few years ago, I had a fantastic remote manager. He would have been a fantastic manager anywhere, though - there wasn't anything especially important about the remote part. He was detailed, friendly, hard-working, and most of all he acted in good faith. That's not to say everything was perfect, but as far as managing a large number of people, it's safe to say this guy was doing a great job.

As far as personality goes, him and I couldn't have been further apart. If he was the moon, I was the Mariana Trench. If he was a kale salad, I was a greasy breakfast at Waffle House. That doesn't bode well for my own chops as a remote manager, but I learned some important things from him that I try to emulate in our own company.

First, he was an excellent listener. Although I'm not bad at listening (most introverted types are innately good at taking a back seat and listening to other people talk) there's always room to grow.

Second, he was supremely analytical. I'm much more of a gut feeling sort of person - my intuition is pretty decent, but I've learned more than once that I shouldn't ever rely on it solely when it comes to important, career-pivoting sorts of decisions.

Third, he was very process-oriented. I did not come out of the womb a very process-oriented person, but it's been a long evolutionary arc of learning to love the spreadsheet.

Fourth, he documented exhaustively. This is one thing, at least, I'm really good at. I write a lot.

Fifth, he was affable. I'm not known as the most affable guy. Friendly, sure. Outgoing and able to chat, sure. Affable? Not quite so much. If only there was a button to change parts of your personality, right?

And sixth, he was extremely eloquent and graceful. Eloquence and grace are like myths to me. They might as well be the lost city of Atlantis. I've heard it exists somewhere under the ocean, but don't depend on me to tell you where it is.

All of these characteristics are important when you're managing a remote team, because through your various forms of communication (email, chat, video meetings, phone calls) every little part of the manager is amplified. Does he make people laugh in real life? In a remote role he would be the manager comedian. Is he slightly obnoxious in real life? In a remote role he is the annoying guy everyone somehow forgets to acknowledge whenever he joins the video call. Is he an obsessive perfectionist? His emails will be enough to send his peons scattering in fear to their therapists.

One of the most important things to keep in mind when you're managing remote employees is that trust is paramount. You've got a gulf separating yourself from your team, usually both physically and chronologically. If you can't trust your team to make independent, self-directed decisions, you can't expect to find any level of success in your remote projects.

Similarly, the employees in your organization must trust the rest of their team, along with the hierarchy above them.

A hands-off approach is essential, because there is no practical way to have constant monitoring and analysis of your team's activity short of a live video feed directly into their room. Believe it or not, that's an approach that's been used more than once, even if it's creepy and laughable.

Developing a company culture that encourages independence and creativity is incredibly crucial to a successful remote team. This is a complex long-term project that might be above the pay grade of the average team member or department manager, but it's essential nonetheless.

Remote work doesn't implement well when you're using antiquated approaches to business culture. You can't really expect a team of suited-up

MBAs with a corporate history at Goldman Sachs or PricewaterhouseCoopers to make up your perfect remote team.

You're inevitably going to have a team of misfits and adventurers, who've had some strange career paths and educational pursuits.

And that's just fine.

An Afterword

As I mentioned in the very beginning of this book, throughout the course of human history working from home has always been the norm, rather than the exception. But remote work is a little different than working from home. There is an added dimension of being able to marry productivity with travel, and it's revolutionized the way people think about work.

A steady, solid remote career is possible. And it's not only possible to have a steady career, but it's possible to have a *thriving* career. When I started working remotely, a few years after college, I was a freelancer mainly concerned with making rent on time each month. Over a decade of remote work since then, and my wife and I have been able to see the same level of success than we would have had in a traditional job (or perhaps even more). We've had the freedom to quit our jobs, start a company, travel to dozens of countries, buy a house, hire employees, and still manage to relax and grab a couple drinks on the weekend.

Remote work has spawned a cornucopia of new ideas and new processes, some of them frustrating, some of them delusional, and some of them a massive improvement upon the status quo. It has spawned an industry of travel influencers, balancing laptops upon that pair of well-tanned legs, battling the blazing glare of the sun on a beach somewhere in the South Pacific. It has spawned a revolution in expectations from people working in tech, marketing, or related information industries.

Chances are, if you work behind a computer screen most of the time, your job can function in an either entirely or partially remote manner.

And for those of you who manage remote employees, or are playing with the idea of going remote yourself, learning how to deal with the intricacies of distributed work is essential.

The question isn't so much *if* this will happen, but *when*.

About the Author

Gil Gildner is an author and cofounder based in Northwest Arkansas.

For several years, Gil worked as a freelance media consultant for nonprofit organizations, carrying a bag of camera gear throughout Europe, Africa, Latin America, and Asia. After this, Gil worked as the director of special projects for a fully remote startup, marketing luxury airfare and documenting a round-the-world trip with 18 flights in 40 days.

With his wife, Anya, he cofounded Discosloth, an entirely remote search marketing & web analytics consulting company with employees in both North America and Europe. He has authored *Becoming A Digital Marketer*, and *The Beginner's Guide To Google Ads*.

He works from home, and has traveled to over 45 countries.

You can find his website at gilgildner.com.

CPSIA information can be obtained
at www.ICGtesting.com
Printed in the USA
LVHW041540160120
643871LV00003B/344

9 781733 794817